IMAGES
of America

Crowell Hilaka and the Richfield Heritage Preserve

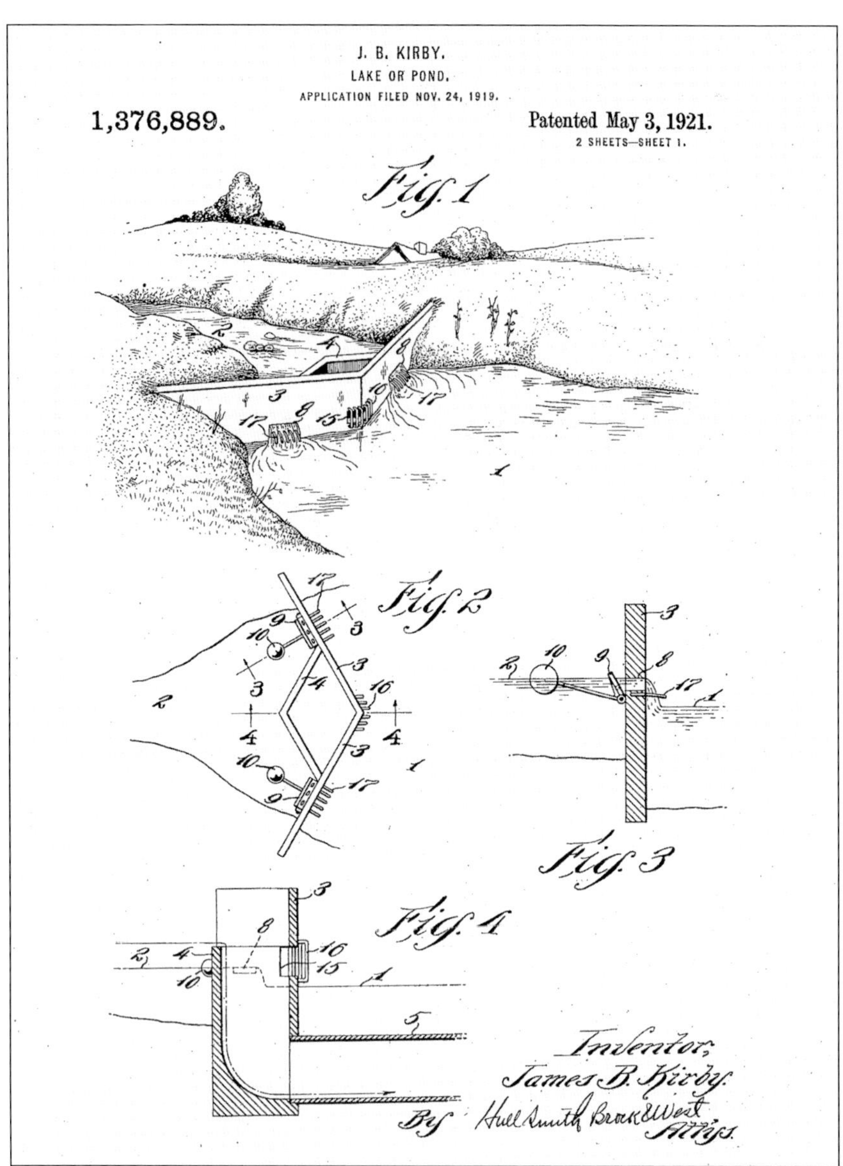

This is the first page of Jim Kirby's patent application for his clear-water lake, showing an upstream intake dam. The system worked by diverting silt-bearing high water from storms or spring thaws into drains under the lake to be discharged below the main retaining dam. Kirby applied for the patent in 1919 after he had begun the installation of the system at his new home in Richfield, Ohio. (Courtesy of US Patent and Trademark Office.)

On the Cover: It was all about the water. Girl Scouts swim in Jim Kirby's patented lake during summer resident camp around 1940. Construction of this lake was the first major project Kirby worked on after he purchased this property in 1919. When the Cleveland Girl Scouts were looking for a campground, "a good lake" was their main criterion. Protection of this lake was the reason they also purchased the Neal estate in 1957, which was then appropriately named Hilaka, "the High Lake." (Courtesy of Girl Scouts of North East Ohio.)

IMAGES
of America

Crowell Hilaka and the Richfield Heritage Preserve

Lynn Scholle Richardson

ISBN 978-1-4671-0703-7

Published by Arcadia Publishing
Charleston, South Carolina

Printed in the United States of America

Library of Congress Control Number: 2021935804

For all general information, please contact Arcadia Publishing:
Telephone 843-853-2070
Fax 843-853-0044
E-mail sales@arcadiapublishing.com
For customer service and orders:
Toll-Free 1-888-313-2665

Visit us on the Internet at www.arcadiapublishing.com

To my husband, Rob Richardson, who founded Friends of Crowell Hilaka in 2009. He has been my mainstay, best road-trip buddy, and favorite tech-support guru while writing this book.

Contents

Acknowledgments

My deepest gratitude is for the people of Richfield who chose to buy the old Girl Scout camp and thereby saved it from destruction. When I think back on that time, I still marvel at the number of people and organizations who came together to make it possible. The Richfield Historical Society was the seed that preserved core information on Jim Kirby and the Oviatt family, which was crucial for the preservation of the property. The effort would have come to naught without the Western Reserve Land Conservancy, Friends of Crowell Hilaka, Buckeye Trail Association, Jane Christyson of Girl Scouts of North East Ohio (GSNEO), Richfield Township, the Village of Richfield, and the many Richfield Together donors and campaign workers.

This book was only possible because of the many, many camp alumni who were willing to share their pictures and memories and who supported Friends of Crowell Hilaka. Whether or not their name appears in this book, they all contributed some aspect to understanding the history of Richfield Heritage Preserve. Archeological studies of the site by Dr. Phil Wanyerka of Cleveland State University; historical research by Rich Sicha and Marcia Moll for the National Register of Historic Places; and Chris Naizer, FoCH's Facebook editor who I rely on for breaking news—all have provided valuable insights. Laura Kirby Cronin, Barbara Neal Sandford, Bruce Leech, Ray and Joann Oviatt, and Garlen Oviatt all contributed family pictures and stories and were delightful hosts and storytellers. To advance readers Sunny Baddour, Sherry Petkovsek, Karen Smik, Team Norris (Pat, Sandy, and Carrie), and my title manager, Caroline Vickerson, at Arcadia, your commentary was much appreciated, even though I sometimes argued. To special agents/angels Corey, Karen, and Nancy: I would not have made it through the winter without you. Finally, I would like to thank my mother-in-law Ele Richardson, who knows all manner of camp songs and folklore and talked me into becoming a Girl Scout volunteer in 1977. The involvement snowballed. These stories would not have come to light without you.

During much of the time period covered by this brief history, there are few records. For other times, there is such an abundance of photographs that it was extremely difficult to choose which ones to include. There are many stories yet to discover, and some may change our understanding of the history of Richfield Heritage Preserve. Meanwhile, any omissions and errors are my own.

INTRODUCTION

Richfield Heritage Preserve is a hidden treasure with layers of history that were sealed away from the surrounding community for over a generation. Home to pioneers and entrepreneurs, the land became the premier camp of the Cleveland Girl Scout Council in 1937. Thousands of young women had their first adventures away from home here, and it is said that the echo of their laughter and their songs can still be heard in the quiet of the woods. Now a public park, the site is listed in the National Register of Historic Places by its "camp name": the Camp Crowell Hilaka Historic District. Its 336 acres inspire passion and energy as it continues to evolve.

The story of the park starts with prehistoric Native Americans who made at least temporary camps here. When the Europeans arrived, competing claims over the rich but uncharted territory of the Ohio lands led to clashes amongst themselves and against the tribes already here. After the American Revolutionary War, the State of Connecticut maintained its "Western Reserve" claim in northeast Ohio. In 1795, Connecticut sold the land to the Connecticut Land Company, which in turn divided it and sold portions to investors and settlers.

In 1811, Heman Oviatt got a deal on buying the entire northwest quadrant of Richfield Township. The previous owner had bought the land as an investment, but he decided to cut his losses and sell out. War was on the horizon as the native tribes were uniting and aligning with the British to take back their land. Property that would have commanded between $4–5 an acre was going for $1.25. Oviatt was the mayor of Hudson, owner of a profitable trading post, and benefactor of the new Western Reserve College. Now he had become a major landowner, and he invited his large family back in Connecticut to come west and settle in the new land. Most of them did.

Among the Oviatt clan who settled in Richfield was Heman's young nephew Mason. In 1831, Mason Oviatt married Fanny Abia Carter, and they settled on 100 acres of what would become Richfield Heritage Preserve. Their farm was handed down through three generations to their grandson Raymond. In 1919, when Ray and his wife were ready to retire from farming and move into town, they sold their land to James B. Kirby.

Kirby was an inventor from Cleveland who had just made his fortune. When he moved to Richfield, he transformed the land with his exuberant creativity. He constructed what is the world's only known patented lake. He took an ancient gristmill design and adapted it for producing electricity in a low-flow stream. His workshop, where he continued to invent, was on the second floor of the mill. He built a relatively simple house that he air-conditioned with spring water, and he built a dance hall on streetcar springs. He made trails and trout ponds, a garden, and a boat launch. Then he bought up the surrounding farms until he had 243 acres. After 15 years, he moved a short distance up the road to construct a bigger house and a larger lake. His old estate, he sold to the Cleveland Girl Scout Council. He even lowered the price of the land so that the Girl Scouts could afford it. This land became Camp Julia Crowell.

In those preelectronic years, camping was the mainstay of the Girl Scout program. A prospectus for the 1937 drive to buy the camp stated, "For the city-bred Scouts, no part of the program is more important than camping. Not only does it teach girls how to take care of themselves under primitive, natural conditions, but it provides simple, adventurous activities out-of-doors in the adolescent years." Camping was wildly popular, and Camp Julia Crowell was usually filled to capacity.

Then in 1957, the Neal family, who owned the land adjacent to the camp, offered their property to the Girl Scouts. This precipitated a crisis, for the council had already tapped all its capital three years previously to buy the land for a second camp. But the Neal property was too good to pass up. It, too, was purchased and became Camp Hilaka. Its graceful houses inspired the realization that Crowell Hilaka was no ordinary camp and could be a world-class destination.

In the 1960s, the Girl Scouts added a larger dining hall, a swimming pool, and a new entrance. In the 1970s, a perimeter fence and locked gates were placed around the entire property to protect the girls, but they contributed to the disconnect between the camp and the surrounding neighborhoods. In the 1980s, the council added a permanent horse stable and year-round program staff. In the 1990s, the council added high-ropes and low-ropes challenge courses.

As changes in society and technology unfolded, "going to camp" was sometimes seen as a challenge instead of a cultural norm. The prevalence of air-conditioning meant there was less of a drive toward getting away to the deep woods or the lakeside to stay cool. The continuous availability of video entertainment made going outside to play less universal. Rising costs of liability and compliance with increased regulation forced camp owners to raise their prices. This made camp too expensive for some families. With fewer participants, Girl Scout councils had to make program cuts, which led to a downward spiral of still fewer participants. At the dawn of the 21st century, the national Girl Scouting organization (GSUSA) began a complete reassessment of its services, followed by an operational and program overhaul. Recognition that children played outside less, were less willing to tolerate "primitive conditions," and had more options for leisure activities prompted GSUSA to broaden its programs and to encourage councils toward "fewer, but better" camping facilities. Crowell Hilaka was one of many camps across the county to be closed.

In 2014, the citizens of Richfield voted to purchase Crowell Hilaka. In 2016, it was renamed Richfield Heritage Preserve to honor its historical legacies.

Richfield resident Peg Couch notes, "I remember us passing by the entrance to the Girl Scout camp and seeing station wagons filled with other young girls like myself on their way to camp there. You often could hear them singing campfire songs! Oh, how I wanted to go inside there and see what I thought would be the most fun part of being a Girl Scout. I was a member of a Girl Scout troop, but we were not allowed to go there as we belonged to a different district. We all had fun, but the mystery of Crowell Hilaka always haunted me. It was so close but seemed so very far away. Now I am in my late 60s and in a wheelchair but have been to Richfield Heritage Preserve and am in awe of the beauty and history of this special place. Now I know that the grass is greener on the other side of that fence. And we are now all welcome to come through the entrance and see the magic inside. It is more wonderful than I even dared to imagine!"

One

The Oviatt Family

The 11 children of the Oviatt family in Goshen, Connecticut, grew up hearing the story of how their mother had been captured by Indians as a young girl and released after seven months. Her brother Nathan, who had been captured with her, was adopted into the tribe. Eventually, Nathan's son, the Oviatt children's half-white, half-native cousin, became a prominent member of the Cherokee Nation. In 1800, Heman Oviatt, the eldest brother, took his wife, Eunice, and their two small sons west with the David Hudson party to settle in the wilds of Connecticut's Western Reserve in the Ohio Lands. They set up a trading post and were known to be sympathetic to the natives. Eunice became fluent in three tribal languages and once even took the side of natives against whites in a court trial.

Perhaps these sympathies help explain why Heman thought it would be a good idea to buy over 5,000 acres of land in nearby Richfield when the previous owner was getting out before the "Indians" took over. Or why most of the rest of the Connecticut Oviatts thought it would be a good idea to join him just as the native tribes were banding together to assist the British in what would become the War of 1812. Or maybe they were hungry enough for new land that they were willing to take the risk.

Heman's brother Salmon came with his wife, Mary, and their 11 children. One of those children was Mason. When Mason grew up, he married Fanny Carter, and they continued in the family tradition of having 11 children. Mason bought a 100-acre parcel of land in Richfield from his parents. It was in a valley at the western edge of the township. It was there that he dammed up the creek, a tributary to the Rocky River, and built a sawmill in 1834. At the mill, he fashioned the lumber for his house, which he finished in 1836.

Meanwhile, the patriarch of the family, Uncle Heman, was involved with abolitionist John Brown. Brown moved to Richfield. Connections were made. Mason was recruited to help transport people escaping slavery.

Heman Oviatt came to the Ohio Western Reserve in 1800 when it was still a "howling wilderness." A successful trader with the native tribes, he became the first mayor of Hudson Township. He endowed the first professorship at Western Reserve College, later Case Western Reserve University. He bought the northwest quadrant of Richfield Township and encouraged his many relatives back in Connecticut to settle on his land in Ohio. This portrait of Oviatt was painted by Allen Smith Jr. (Courtesy of Case Western Reserve University Archives.)

John Brown came to live in Richfield in 1842 to work off a debt he owed to Heman Oviatt. Later, he became famous when he attempted to lead a slave insurrection starting with the capture of a US Army arsenal at Harper's Ferry, Virginia, one of the events contributing to the American Civil War. While still living in Richfield, Brown worked with Mason Oviatt to carry escaping slaves to Oberlin. According to family tradition, Mason built a false floor in the bottom of his wagon so that the escapees could hide underneath, and then a load of hay was piled on top. (Courtesy of Library of Congress.)

Richfield 3d January 1842

It is the mutual understanding of the undersigned that Heman Oviatt is to purchase Hides and Calf Skins of a good quality during the present year and that John Brown is to receive them, Tan and finish them in a neat and workmanlike manner rendering to said Oviatt all the leather made from the same in good order, or pay for any damage they may receive while in his particular care. and that said Oviatt shall account with said Brown for nine twentyeths of the wholesale value of all leather so delivered by applying it towards cancelling the debt due from said Brown to said Oviatt.

And that [illegible] O M Oviatt shall hereafter discontinue the business of tanning upon shares and let said Brown have that kind of custom in their place untill a different arangement shall be made between them, and that said Brown shall render to said O M Oviatt every assistance, information, or other facility in his power to afford in the management of his Tanary or any other branch of said O M Oviatts business about which said Brown may be possessed of proper information

Heman Oviatt

John Brown

Orrin M. Oviatt

This contract states that John Brown will process hides for the Oviatts until his debt to them is cleared. While working for the Oviatts in Richfield, Brown's wife and children contracted a serious illness and were cared for by neighbors, including Fanny Oviatt. Four of the children died and were buried in the East Richfield cemetery. (Courtesy of Boyd B. Sutler Collection, West Virginia State Archives.)

Heman Oviatt's nephew Mason Oviatt bought 100 acres in what is now the southern third of Richfield Heritage Preserve. With his brother Erastus, he built a sawmill on the site in 1834 to shape the boards for his house as well as provide some extra income. In 1836, he finished this house situated on the corner of what is now State Route 303 and Oviatt Road. A solid structure, it housed three generations of the Oviatt family. After they left, it was home to Kirby's tenant farmers and then a succession of Girl Scout camp managers. (Courtesy of Rob Richardson.)

Mason Oviatt joined the great Summit County cavalcade heading overland to California, looking to strike it rich in the Gold Rush. He died there, and his body was returned home for burial in the West Richfield Cemetery. Fanny was left with their eight remaining children. At that time, Sarah was 17 years old, Amanda was 14, Fanny Louise was 13, Miles was 9, Electa was 6, Truman was 4, Helen was 2, and Chloe was 16 months old. (Courtesy of Richfield Historical Society.)

Fanny Oviatt never remarried. She signed ownership of the farm over to Mason's brother Uri, who lived nearby, but she continued to live in their house, run the farm, and pay taxes on both in Mason's name until 1870. According to historian Eunice Merton, "Fanny was a schoolteacher in the neighboring town of Bath. She was her own janitor, cleaning the schoolroom each night and caring for the fire. The school directors furnished the wood. Wherever she went, she took her flax wheel with her. It was with money earned from her spinning that she bought her clothes and other incidentals. The school directors called on her to claim her earnings from this source. She drew herself up in indignation and told them what she did after four o'clock in the afternoon and before nine in the morning was her business. This was considered a very brave thing to do. That winter, her father's oxen died, and she took the money earned from her spinning and bought him a new yoke of oxen." (Courtesy of Richfield Historical Society.)

While the family farm was passed down to Mason and Fanny's grandson Raymond, the family stories were passed down to their granddaughter Jenny Farwell Oviatt (left). Jenny told the stories to her friend Eunice Merton (right), a highly respected businesswoman and historian nationally known for the accuracy and lyricism of her seasonal weather predictions. From time to time, Merton published dramatized aspects of Fanny's oral history in her column in the Brecksville newspaper, the *Gristmill*. (Left, courtesy of Richfield Historical Society; right, courtesy of Bob Hooper.)

The Oviatt clan sat for this photograph at a family gathering in 1902. Mason and Fanny's son Miles is seated second from the left in the first row of adults, next to his wife, Permilla, who is holding a baby. Miles and Permilla's son Raymond is standing in the fourth row, third from the left. It was Raymond who inherited the old Oviatt farm and sold it to Jim Kirby in 1919. (Courtesy of Richfield Historical Society.)

Two

Inventor Jim Kirby

A self-taught engineer and inventor, James Blaine Kirby made the landscape of Richfield Heritage Preserve what it is today. He created a patented, clear-water lake that he named Jinelle—a combination of his first name with that of his wife, Nellie. His iconic mill was an experiment in hydroelectric generation on a low-flow stream. The dance hall on springs was another successful experiment. His second upstream lake inspired his neighbors, the Neals, to build their houses on its shores. Kirby arranged the roads and trails through his land for recreation instead of farming. Finally, he sold the land to the Cleveland Girl Scout Council for far less than its value so that children could benefit from it. He financed all this with his many successful inventions designed to "eliminate the drudgery of housework."

Kirby granted few interviews during his lifetime, and those were mostly associated with business pursuits: the introduction of the eponymous Kirby Vacuum Cleaner around 1935, the Apex "bouncing basket" washing machine in 1947, and the 1956 opening of Oceanside Shopping Center, which he developed in Pompano Beach, Florida. At the time of this writing, it is not known why Kirby left the land that he loved. It is known that at first, he stayed in Richfield. Nellie had mobility issues, and the new house was the first in Richfield to have an elevator. It may be that he had a hankering to try out new construction ideas or that he needed an expanse of flat grazing land for the herd of prize cattle that he developed. After Nellie's death in 1961, Kirby moved permanently to Florida, where he lived in the penthouse of his Oceanside Apartments building.

Jim Kirby was born in Cleveland in 1884 and died in Fort Lauderdale, Florida, in 1971. He amassed 162 American patents, most to improvements in household appliances. He was inspired by observing his mother's toil at endless housework chores and devoted himself to inventing machines that could do such repetitive chores for her. (Courtesy of Richfield Historical Society.)

WIZARD.

West-Side Has a Young and Tender Edison.

Cleveland has a 13-year-old boy who bids fair to astonish the world as an inventor and electrician.

This singularly gifted boy's name is Jas. B. Kirby. He is a son of Jas. D. Kirby, of 54 Marvin-av.

JAS. B. KIRBY.

Master Kirby is a born electrician. He presents the only known instance of a child born with a knowledge of electricity. But a little over a year ago, when the first principles were explained to him, the boy seemed to understand them intuitively.

Among the long list of inventions for which Master Kirby is responsible is a telegraph instrument, galvanometer, magnets, induction coil, double carbon electric light and a microphone. It is claimed that the last named instrument will carry the voice 2000 miles. Young Kirby has just completed a motor, which is a complete success, and he is at present engaged upon a 16-cell battery. Young Kirby is known among his friends and associates as the

As a boy, Jim took a YMCA class called "Electricity and Magic" that changed his life. This clipping from an unidentified Cleveland newspaper in 1898 outlines his abilities with electrical devices and growing reputation as the "Wizard of the West Side." (Courtesy of Richfield Historical Society.)

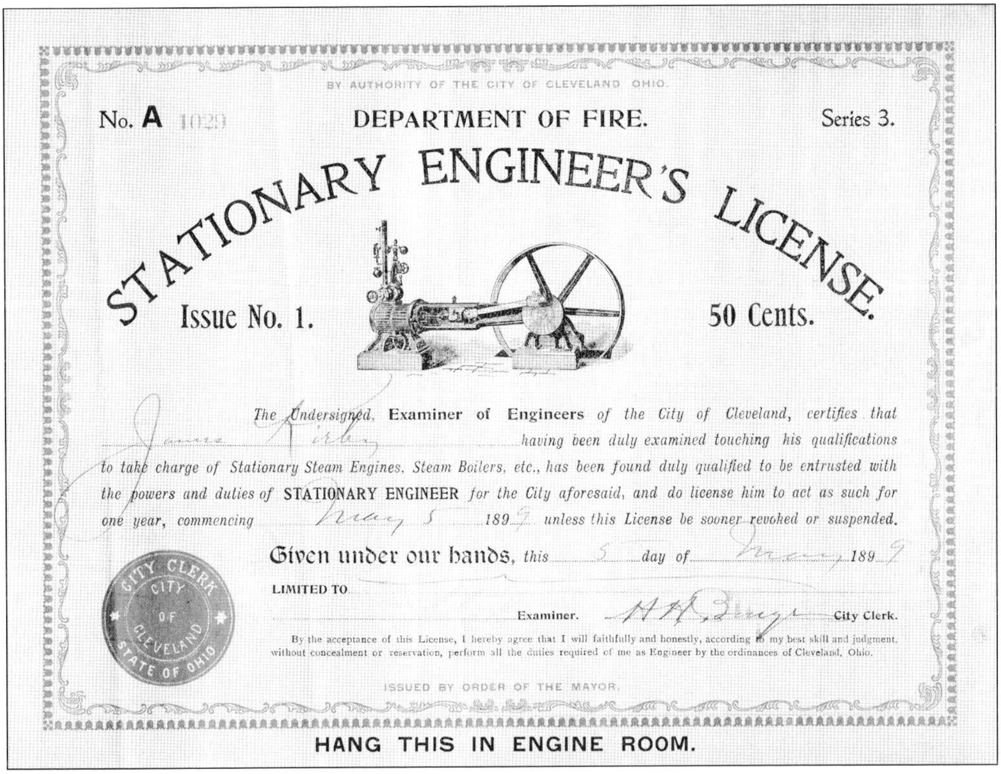

BY AUTHORITY OF THE CITY OF CLEVELAND OHIO.

No. A 1029 DEPARTMENT OF FIRE. Series 3.

STATIONARY ENGINEER'S LICENSE.

Issue No. 1. 50 Cents.

The Undersigned, Examiner of Engineers of the City of Cleveland, certifies that James Kirby having been duly examined touching his qualifications to take charge of Stationary Steam Engines, Steam Boilers, etc., has been found duly qualified to be entrusted with the powers and duties of STATIONARY ENGINEER for the City aforesaid, and do license him to act as such for one year, commencing May 5 1899 unless this License be sooner revoked or suspended.

Given under our hands, this 5 day of May 1899

LIMITED TO

Examiner. City Clerk.

CITY CLERK CITY OF CLEVELAND STATE OF OHIO

By the acceptance of this License, I hereby agree that I will faithfully and honestly, according to my best skill and judgment, without concealment or reservation, perform all the duties required of me as Engineer by the ordinances of Cleveland, Ohio.

ISSUED BY ORDER OF THE MAYOR.

HANG THIS IN ENGINE ROOM.

In 1899, at the age of 14, he was awarded a stationary steam operator's license. In interviews, Kirby reminisced that his eighth-grade teacher assigned him to build a working model of a gristmill. "It really wasn't much of a flour mill," he said. "But it worked." (Courtesy of Laura Kirby Cronin.)

Kirby's mother, Sylvia Bigelow Kirby, was the inspiration for his success as an inventor. He had watched her seemingly endless toil of housework and laundry and believed he could harness the power of machines and electricity to make her life easier. (Courtesy of Laura Kirby Cronin.)

As an adult, Jim Kirby kept a sense of playfulness, as shown when he was caught climbing this tree in Boston Township. He once stopped his chauffeur-driven limousine as it drove past the general store in Richfield (now the Doug Out Pub & Grill) to join a group of children in their marbles game. (Courtesy of Richfield Historical Society.)

The wedding of James B. Kirby to his first wife, Hazel Hackett, took place in 1909. Hazel grew up on a farm in Bath Township and became a schoolteacher there. Jim and Hazel became frequent visitors to the Hackett farm. (Courtesy of Laura Kirby Cronin.)

Jim Kirby is shown standing in the back with his arm extended as he and his Bigelow relatives plan for the first reunion of the Bigelow cousins in 1914. His mother, Sylvia, is standing in the back row on the right. This remarkable family included Lena Bigelow Stouffer, whose apple pies grew into Stouffer's Frozen Foods, and Herb Bigelow, who started Bigelow Motors. (Courtesy of Richfield Historical Society.)

Kirby made it his life's goal to eliminate the drudgery of housework. The Franz Premier Company was formed to manufacture and sell Kirby's first vacuum cleaners for home use around 1910. (Author's collection.)

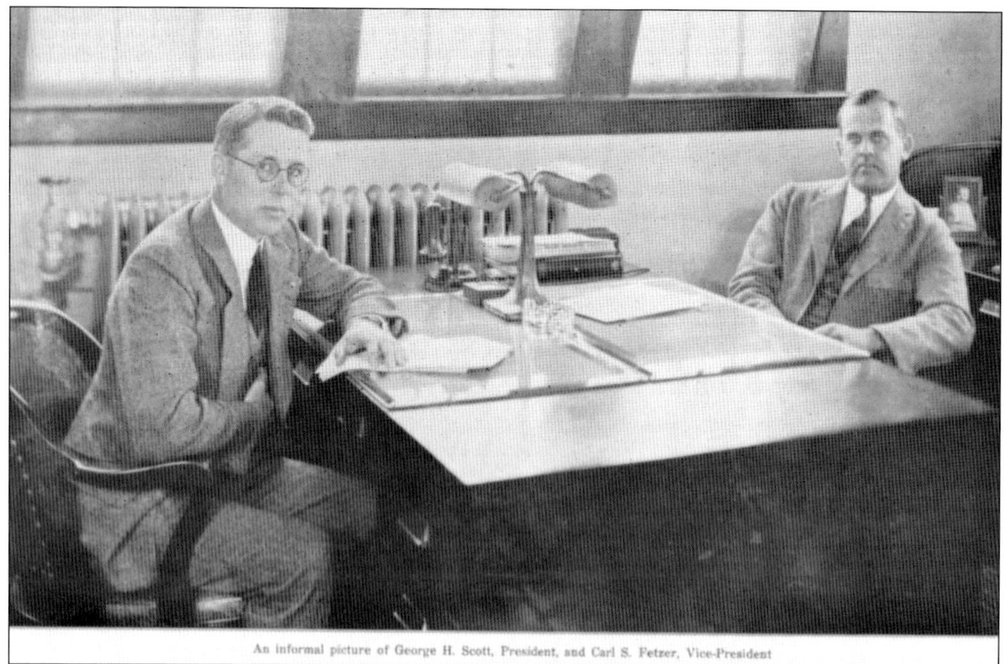

In 1918, Jim Kirby met his future partners George Scott (left) and Carl Fetzer (right) when he helped them retool their machine shop to produce Very pistol flare guns for the war. After the war, Scott and Fetzer began making and selling Kirby's nonelectric vacuum cleaners for rural households in a spin-off subsidiary company they called Vacuette. (Courtesy of Richfield Historical Society.)

Walter Kirby (left) and his older brother Jim (standing right) proudly display the rabbits they had shot at the Hackett Farm. Later, Jim turned against hunting and developed a plan for a "bloodless fox hunt" (not realizing that such events had existed in England since the mid-1800s). It was not popular with his friends, and Jim dubbed it his "least successful invention." (Courtesy of Laura Kirby Cronin.)

From left to right, Jim Kirby and his brothers-in-law Claire and Miller Hackett pose with Kirby's prototype wringerless washing machine in front of the Hackett's chicken coop around 1915. The motor for this test model was positioned about eight feet away from the washing machine. (Courtesy of Laura Kirby Cronin.)

Newton Hackett posed with his flock of chickens while the laundry done in his son-in-law's newfangled device finished drying on the clothesline behind him. Kirby greatly admired his in-laws' farm in Bath Township. When he decided to buy a farm of his own, the Oviatt farm in nearby Richfield had the topography he needed. (Courtesy of Laura Kirby Cronin.)

A spin-cycle washing machine was Jim Kirby's breakthrough invention that made his fortune. His washing machine eliminated the need for a separate wringing process, which was heavy and sometimes dangerous work. Here, Kirby is shown with a prototype model in the factory gearing up to produce the washers he called "LaunDRYette." (Courtesy of Laura Kirby Cronin.)

The LaunDRYette was extremely successful. The money Kirby made from this invention allowed him to buy an estate in the country. (Author's collection.)

What More Appreciated Gift for Christmas than THE LAUN-DRY-ETTE for Wash-day Problems?

The Only Electric Washing Machine Made That Does Not Require a Wringer.

IMAGINE, if you can, the comfort of feeling that regardless of the weather—yes, or the Laundress—that the washing and ironing can all be finished and put away in half the time that it takes the old way.

The operation of the machine is a marvel of simplicity—impossible to make a mistake, or cause injury in its operation. The power for driving both the washer and dryer is controlled by the same lever, the change in position of the inside tub causing the machine to perform the character of service desired. All moving parts that might cause injury are underneath and protected by a metal shield.

The LAUN-DRY-ETTE is the only washing machine on the market that does not require a wringer. It dries the clothes without the use of either a hand or power wringer, eliminating for all time the many disadvantages attendant upon the use of this device. By pressing the foot pedal down it raises the inside tub, which automatically starts it revolving, forcing the water through the perforations into the outside tub. The clothes come from the dryer unwrinkled, buttons intact, color unaffected, with just enough moisture evenly distributed to make ironing a pleasure.

See Demonstration in Our Store

WE ANNOUNCE AN EXTRAORDINARY
XMAS PRIZE CONTEST
for Boys and Girls
on Page 13 Women's Section

The Stroud-Michael Co.

Retail Store 149 the Old Arcade

Main 4650. Central 8258 K.

The Oviatt farm was blessed with several deep, wooded ravines that could not be plowed or planted but would be perfect for outdoor recreation. In this 1920 photograph of what later became known variously as "the Secret Waterfall" or "Innisfree Falls," Kirby stages a slip on the ice while Hazel, her parents, her brother Claire, and an unidentified child look on and grin. (Courtesy of Laura Kirby Cronin.)

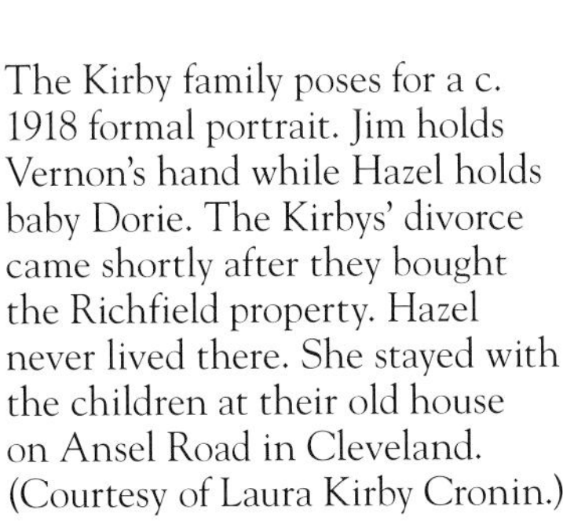

The Kirby family poses for a c. 1918 formal portrait. Jim holds Vernon's hand while Hazel holds baby Dorie. The Kirbys' divorce came shortly after they bought the Richfield property. Hazel never lived there. She stayed with the children at their old house on Ansel Road in Cleveland. (Courtesy of Laura Kirby Cronin.)

This panoramic view of the Kirby estate from the east shore of Lake Jinelle includes Kirby House, a picnic shelter at lake level (later renamed Cricket's Corner), a garage, a springhouse (at center, later known as the Nature Hut), and a dance hall (Garfield Hall). In an astounding six-year surge of creative energy from 1919 to 1924, Jim Kirby purchased the Oviatt farm, constructed the world's first known patented clear-water lake, built a multilevel chalet-style house, erected a picturesque experimental hydroelectric-generating mill, put up a dance hall on retired streetcar

springs, acquired three more farms, and created a second, deeper lake to stock with bigger fish. During this time, he received 22 patents to add to the 29 that he already had. Later, he designed a boathouse and a picnic shelter/boat launch. He planted an apple orchard and hired a botanist to collect wildflowers for his garden. He opened the property to fellow Richfield residents on Mondays and Fridays. (Courtesy of Girl Scouts of North East Ohio.)

The beginnings of Jim Kirby's patented, self-clarifying lake are shown here in 1920. Intake dams on the feeder streams allow normal flow into the lake, but mud-laden stormwater was diverted into drain pipes that carried the muddy water under the lake and discharged it below the main retaining dam. The dam is marked in this picture by the light-colored ramp in the left center of the image. The partly constructed Kirby House is in the background on the right. (Courtesy of Laura Kirby Cronin.)

Logs were cleared by horsepower during the creation of the lake. The old Oviatt farmhouse is in the background. (Courtesy of Laura Kirby Cronin.)

During excavation for the construction of the Lake Jinelle dam in 1919, Kirby found the remnants of Mason Oviatt's old sawmill in roughly the same place. The stumps in the foreground of this picture were still there when the lake was drained for dam repairs in 2019. (Courtesy of Laura Kirby Cronin.)

Water from the secret waterfall flows over the intake dam on the east side of the lake. A wooden bridge was added later. (Courtesy of Richfield Historical Society.)

An unidentified man and dog stand on the bridge below the intake dam on the west side of the lake. The hill in the background would become the site for Kirby's dance hall on springs, later named Garfield Hall. (Courtesy of Richfield Historical Society.)

Jim Kirby is shown paddling here on his patented lake. He loved living near lakes, and all of his adult homes overlooked a body of water, from Rockefeller Lagoon in Cleveland to Mackie Lake in Ontario, to the Atlantic Ocean in Pompano Beach, Florida. At this home in Richfield, he and Nellie had a fine view of Lake Jinelle and the mill from their bedroom windows. (Courtesy of Richfield Historical Society.)

Henry Hammond is shown here with his daughter Marie. It was Hammond's job to go down into the drain pipes under the lake and clean them out. He used a mud sled that Kirby especially designed for this task. (Courtesy of Richfield Historical Society.)

Kirby House was built under the few trees that the Oviatts had left to provide shade in an otherwise cleared field. In 1984, the Girl Scout Council rerouted major repairs of the foundations to save the old white oak seen immediately to the right of the house. The road going behind the house has since overgrown. (Courtesy of Richfield Historical Society.)

Nellie Heller, at right, visited the Hacketts in 1914 when the Kirbys came by with their two-year-old son, Vernon, at left. After Jim Kirby divorced his first wife, he and Nellie were married. Jim named his patented lake Jinelle, a combination of his name and Nellie's. Nellie and Jim remained happily married for 40 years until her death in 1961. (Courtesy of Laura Kirby Cronin.)

Kirby's Mill was patterned after a gristmill but has some unique features. The waterwheel is oriented perpendicularly to the mill house and is mounted on ball bearings so that it could turn with very little water. The original water conduit was positioned underneath the second floor of the mill. (Courtesy of Rob Richardson.)

The waterwheel on Kirby's Mill was an overshot type, where water flows in from the top and into buckets. Waterwheels such as this were actually outdated by the time Kirby built this one in 1922. He may have enjoyed the experimentation, or he may have been nostalgic for the old-fashioned gristmill he had known and modeled as a boy. (Courtesy of Girl Scouts of North East Ohio.)

Jim Kirby is pictured in his workshop on the second floor of the mill while an unidentified helper waits in the loft. The drive belts visible here suggest that some of the machinery may have operated directly off the mechanical power of the turning wheel. A hydroelectric generator was located in the basement and supplied power to the workshop and to the house across the lake. (Courtesy of Richfield Historical Society.)

Kirby's Mill, which he called "the powerhouse," is on the left in this c. 1925 photograph. The curve of the dam wall leads the eye across the road to Kirby's gardens bounded by a split-rail fence, across another road, and then to the orchard on the hillside. A corner of Kirby House is visible on the right. (Courtesy of Girl Scouts of North East Ohio.)

This photograph was taken sometime between 1925 and 1930, judging by the width of tree trunks on the dam and the plantings on the lakeshore. Note the diving platform to the left of center. (Courtesy of Girl Scouts of North East Ohio.)

Jim Kirby was an avid fisherman, as evidenced by this picture postcard of himself (at left) that he sent to his brother from Minnesota in 1914. Although Kirby stocked Lake Jinelle with bluegills, bass, pike, and catfish, he ended up training these fish to come to him so he could scratch their backs, and they became his pets. In a 1936 interview, he said, "I could no more eat one of these fish than I could eat a pet rabbit." (Courtesy of Richfield Historical Society.)

The Vacuette Company described Kirby's dance hall: "On high ground at the head of the lake was built a spacious bungalow, put up especially for the convention, with its deep open fireplace, and polished hardwood floor, where dancing was so easy, to the excellent music of one of Cleveland's best dance orchestras. Adjacent to the bungalow, the big top tent was set and . . . luncheon was served hot from the outdoor stoves." (Courtesy of Special Collections, Michael Schwartz Library, Cleveland State University.)

This back view of the dance hall (later Garfield Hall) shows what it looked like before the Girl Scouts added a kitchen and storage area. The hall was built in 1923 on retired streetcar springs. (Courtesy of Special Collections, Michael Schwartz Library, Cleveland State University.)

Kirby's driveway came in from State Route 303, crossed the creek, and opened out in the meadow below the house. The split-rail fence was there when Kirby bought the property in 1919. Note the road going off to the left, Kirby's Mill on the right, and the concrete parapet at the top of the dam. (Courtesy of Judy Heiser Heit.)

The year "1921" is worked into the stones of the Kirby House's exterior chimney. The stonework was by master stonemason William B. Thompson. (Courtesy of Rob Richardson.)

Fernwood Point is the light-colored rise just right of center across the lake in this image taken by the Heisers in May 1938. In Kirby's time, before the hemlock trees grew on its slopes, Fernwood was a natural lookout point. The Girl Scouts later placed a campsite here. Kirby House is seen on the upper left, and Cricket's Corner is at lake level left of center. (Courtesy of Judy Heiser Heit.)

The Kirbys had a decorative pond and extensive flower garden on the west side of their house. This is the view looking back toward the house in 1926. A report written by the Girl Scout Council in 1942 says that the Kirbys hired a botanist to collect wildflowers from other areas of the county to bring back to their gardens. (Courtesy of Richfield Historical Society.)

Around 1935, the Scott and Fetzer Company formed a spin-off company named after their star inventor. They commissioned an essay by the famous journalist and radio commentator Lowell Thomas. "The Man Who Revolutionized the American Home" was widely distributed as a booklet touting Jim Kirby's inventive genius and gave prospective customers a glimpse into his idyllic estate. (Courtesy of Laura Kirby Cronin.)

In this aerial view of the Kirby estate from 1937, Lake Jinelle is at the bottom (south). Kirby's second lake is at the top, a half a mile upstream. When Kirby considered constructing the upper dam, he recognized that the resulting lake would encroach on the Neals' property. The Neals agreed with Kirby's plan and even paid for one-third of the construction cost. Part of the Neal orchard is easily identifiable by the rows of neat dots in the upper left corner. The hedgerow on the southern border of the field was the boundary between the Neal and Kirby lands and can be followed in a straight line across the lake. (Courtesy of Richfield Historical Society.)

Near the house, between the road and the lake, the Kirbys built a small picnic shelter/boat landing, shown here under construction. Although the shelter is right next to the road, it is tucked into a lower level and sometimes went unnoticed by passersby. (Courtesy of Richfield Historical Society.)

Kirby's first major partner, the Franz Premier Vacuum Cleaner Company, evolved into the Apex Manufacturing Company, makers of home appliances. Jim Kirby was a partner in the company and assigned many of his patents to them. (Author's collection.)

Jim Kirby's partnership with the Scott and Fetzer Company began in 1918. Their early Vacuette Company was rebranded as the Kirby company. The well-known Kirby vacuum cleaners were sold door-to-door. Although he became famous for this, Jim Kirby himself preferred to remain behind the scenes and to work on the continuous improvement of his inventions. (Courtesy of Richfield Historical Society.)

In this c. 1930 Kirby family portrait, Sylvia Bigelow Kirby is seated in the center front, flanked by her sons Jim (left) and Walter (right). Standing in back are Jeanette Kirby (child of Jim), Nellie Heller Kirby (Jim's second wife), Dorie (child of Jim), Vernon (James Vernon, child of Jim), Virginia (child of Walter), Mildred Lovejoy Kirby (Walter's wife), and Arthur (on the pony, child of Walter). (Courtesy of Laura Kirby Cronin.)

Jim Kirby is pictured stepping out of the east door of his home beneath the boughs of the giant white oak. Years later, Girl Scouts would come to love Kirby House. Tina Elkins wrote: "Camp Julia Crowell looked like fairy land. . . . [It] combined the two things I loved most—nature and the world of imagination . . . [and] fed my fantasy life as a "girl out in the woods," often on my own, secure in the safety that the camps offered. I built imaginary villages out of the rocks in the little streams and claimed obscure corners of the camps as my own special places. I escaped imaginary evil racing along the narrow water's edge path around the lower lake to the safety of swing bridge at the mill, or tried to see how fast I could travel the woodland trails that crossed between the two camps. . . . Art is the extension of imagination. All of these things combined helped lead me to art school and a career in the arts." (Courtesy of Girl Scouts of North East Ohio.)

Three

The Cleveland Girl Scout Council

Girl Scouting began in Great Britain when Robert, Lord Baden-Powell founded the wildly popular Boy Scout organization. He soon discovered that there was an overwhelming response from girls who wanted to be a part of it, too. He enlisted his sister Agnes to develop a similar program especially for them. In the first month that the office opened (in 1910), eight thousand Girl Guides registered, including adults leaders. One such adult was an American, Juliet Gordon Low, who was living in Scotland. When she returned home to the United States in 1912, she brought scouting for girls with her.

Girl Scouting grew exponentially over the following years. During World War I, both Boy Scouts and Girl Scouts were pressed into service, helping the home front in any way that they could. One of the tasks of the Girl Scouts in Washington, DC, was to help provide lunches for military and support personnel who flooded into the city.

Pres. Woodrow Wilson appointed a Clevelander, Newton D. Baker, as his secretary of war. Baker, in turn, appointed fellow Clevelander Benedict Crowell as his assistant. When the Baker and Crowell families moved to DC, the two wives wanted to find some way to help the war effort and decided to join the fledging Girl Scout movement. In time, Julia Crowell became commissioner of the Washington Girl Scout Council. Elizabeth Baker became assistant commissioner. At the end of the war, they returned to Cleveland, bringing the Girl Scout organization with them. They convinced their influential friends to help support it. One of the most urgent tasks of the new Cleveland Girl Scout Council was to find a permanent campsite for the girls.

Julia Cobb Crowell grew up on Cleveland's Euclid Avenue, nicknamed "Millionaire's Row." After she married Benedict Crowell in 1904, she and the other society ladies helped each other promote worthy causes. When her husband was tasked with overseeing American production during World War I, Julia went with him to Washington, DC. There, she became involved in the Girl Scouts. (Photograph by George Mountain Edmondson; courtesy of Cleveland Public Library Photograph Collection.)

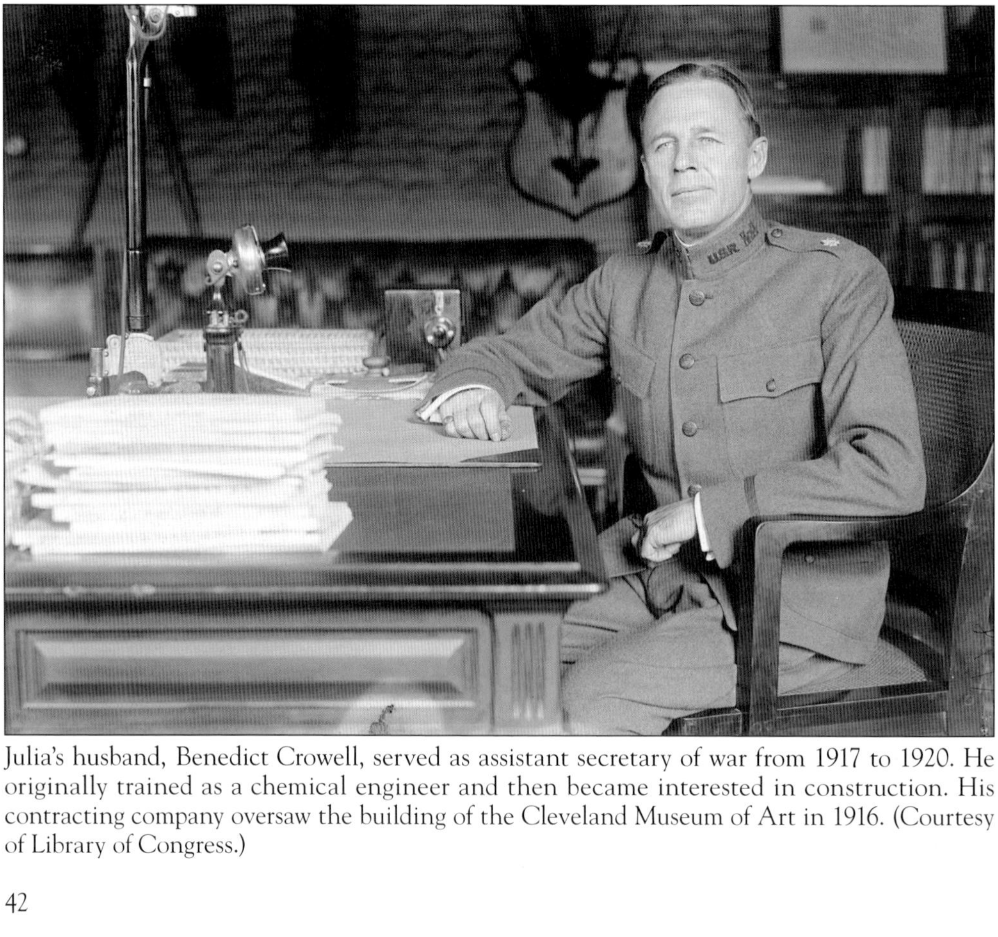

Julia's husband, Benedict Crowell, served as assistant secretary of war from 1917 to 1920. He originally trained as a chemical engineer and then became interested in construction. His contracting company oversaw the building of the Cleveland Museum of Art in 1916. (Courtesy of Library of Congress.)

Julia Crowell (center of photograph, looking toward camera) was the commissioner of the Washington, DC, Girl Scout Council. Surrounded by Scouts in this 1922 photograph, the adults with Crowell are, from left to right, founder of the Girl Scouts of the USA, Juliette Gordon Low; First Lady Florence Harding; and commander of the US Expeditionary Forces in Europe, Gen. John "Black Jack" Pershing. When Crowell returned home to Cleveland, she and her friend Elizabeth Baker started the Cleveland Girl Scout Council. (Courtesy of Library of Congress.)

By 1924, the Cleveland Girl Scout Council had arranged to borrow land of the Hoeret farm near Burton. This undated photograph from Camp Burton showing the girls gathered for all-camp announcements also reveals how platform tents, each with space for four girls, were interspersed among a hillside orchard. The council borrowed this land every summer for 13 years. (Courtesy of Girl Scouts of North East Ohio.)

Even though Camp Burton featured this lovely lake, the council needed land and a lake of its own. Real estate agents showed the Camp Committee innumerable dry farms surrounded by barbed wire fences. Girl Scout historian Georgianna Bonds wrote that "the Camp Committee crawled under so many barbed wire fences that one member finally said she was just 'too old to crawl anymore.' " (Courtesy of Girl Scouts of North East Ohio.)

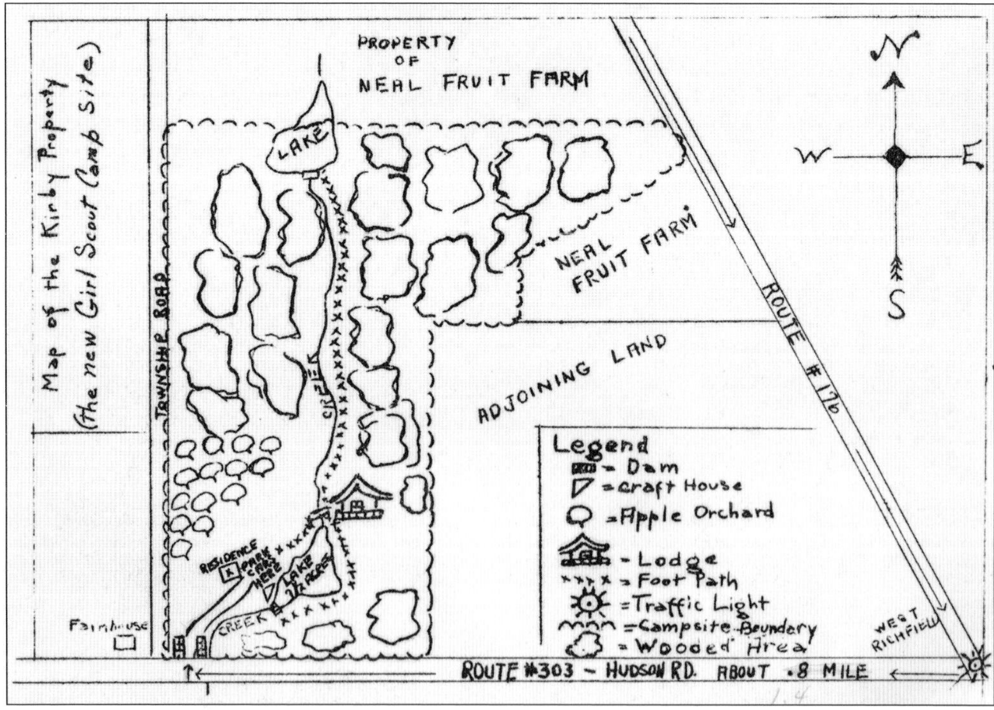

The Camp Committee knew it had crawled under its last barbed-wire fence when they saw the Kirby estate. This quickly drawn map of the property reveals the artist's thoughts: Not only did the property have two lakes with a trail running between them, but it also included a lodge, which could serve as a dining hall, already built and sketched in loving detail. (Courtesy of Girl Scouts of North East Ohio.)

Endorsements for the purchase of the proposed campsite were obtained from First Lady Eleanor Roosevelt, Cleveland safety director Elliot Ness, and feminist writer Abbey Graham, who wrote, "I approve of the sort of campaign you are running in behalf of camping . . . for young eyes to discover the excellence of an adolescent moon . . . whereof some incipient Eve might eat and awaken to a knowledge of her own stupendous importance." (Courtesy of Special Collections, Michael Schwartz Library, Cleveland State University.)

Camp campaign brochures were distributed. Newspapers featured photographic essays, such as one by Alice Kuehn, which began, "In the hills of Ohio, a spot as rustic as the old mill beside the dam and as lovely as the sun when it falls asleep in the arms of West Richfield has been chosen by the Cleveland Girl Scouts for a new camp." (Courtesy of Girl Scouts of North East Ohio.)

After THIRTEEN YEARS . . .

An excellently constructed dam

THE GIRL SCOUTS OF CLEVELAND are ready to realize their dream — an adequate Camp Site in keeping with their excellent record and their acknowledged needs. They ask $60,000 to purchase and equip the proposed Camp Site.

These Facts Stand Out

1. The site, selected after long search, has these great advantages . . . located at West Richfield it is away from the city, but readily accessible . . . it is not *raw* land, but is already improved with buildings adapted to the uses of the Girl Scouts . . . it has sufficient and protected water for drinking, swimming and boating.

2. Permanent possession of this site of 243 acres will make it possible to train 1,400 more girls each year and to take care of younger girls.

3. The new camp site will be open 52 weeks in the year, not a mere 8 weeks as in the past.

4. Present facilities make it impossible for all the agencies for girls to serve more than 10 per cent of the girls in Cuyahoga county.

5. Cleveland is the only city in the region that does not own its own Girl Scout camp.

6. Figures from Akron, Dayton, Cincinnati, Toledo and Columbus show that the cost of the total set-up is less than those cities have had to pay.

The lodge for eating and recreation

The millhouse is perfect for craft work

The seven acre lake with its beach will make possible expert training in swimming, rowing and canoeing

The 11 room, heated house makes winter week ends possible

A gas well on the property provides both fuel and a small income

THE CLEVELAND PRESS

Girl Scouts Launch Campaign to Raise $60,000 to Buy Camp Site

Pictured here are Cleveland Girl Scout leaders as they met last night in the University Club to open a fund campaign for a new camp site.

Among those shown, Prof. Busch is associate director of Cleveland College and was principal speaker at the meeting; Mrs. Friede is Cleveland Girl Scout commissioner; Mr. Madison is director of the Cleveland Museum of Natural History; Mrs. Bates is second deputy Girl Sc commissioner; Mr. Seely is campaign chairman; Mrs. Bonfils was c man for the dinner which preceded the meeting; Mr. Green is Scout executive; Mrs. McQuate is first deputy commissioner, and Wright is Cleveland Girl Scout director.

The public fundraising campaign kicked off with a banquet at the University Club in Cleveland. This *Cleveland Press* collage depicting that event features many familiar names. Jim Kirby sits next to Julia Crowell in the upper-left segment. In the top-middle segment is Linnea Friede, for whom Lake Linnea was later named. In the upper right is Harold Madison, director of the Cleveland Museum of Natural History and chairman of the Camp Planning Committee. Below Madison is Warner Seely, chairman of the Camp Fundraising Committee. Next to Seely is Margaret Bates. In the lower-left segment is Eleanor Garfield. In three weeks' time, the Girl Scouts raised the money they needed from 5,050 individuals "from every corner of Cuyahoga County." Donations ranged from 10¢ to $10,000. Coincidently, publicity for the campaign was handled by Eleanor Farnham. Farnham's ancestral home in Richfield was built by "Lord" Everett Farnham, who married Eleanor Oviatt, a cousin of Mason Oviatt and Ruth Oviatt Freeman. (Courtesy of Special Collections, Michael Schwartz Library, Cleveland State University.)

Four

Camp Julia Crowell

The Girl Scouts received the title to their new camp on April 1, 1937.

The Kirbys' house would be the administrative headquarters and infirmary for summer camp. It would serve as a cabin for troop camping the rest of the year. The mill would become an arts and crafts studio.

The Kirbys' tenant farmer, Henry Heiser, would stay on as the camp handyman and continue living with his family in the old Oviatt farmhouse.

A kitchen and storage area were built on the back of the dance hall so that it could double as the dining hall. A screened porch was added to the front so girls would have a protected space to wait before entering. A small cabin was constructed nearby for the cook.

Space was cleared for seven tent units: Orchard Way, Beechcliff, Fernwood, Glencairn, Hickory Hill, Windy Hill, and Innisfree. Tent platforms were built. Latrine pits were dug, and outhouses were constructed over them.

Camp was open for business that July.

In August, when the pace of adjustment had slowed, the dining hall was dedicated as Garfield Hall in honor of Eleanor Garfield, the second commissioner of the Cleveland Girl Scout Council. The Kirbys' former home was officially dedicated as Kirby House.

A year-round reforestation program was begun under the direction of Helen Banta, nature counselor, in consultation with Roy Patten, forester from the Ohio Agricultural Experimental Station in Wooster.

It was all going wonderfully. But within a few years, as more girls became Scouts, the popular camp did not have enough room to accommodate everyone who wanted to stay there.

The dedication of Camp Julia Crowell took place on June 20, 1937. The raising of the flag took place on the terrace across from the spring-loaded dance hall converted into a dining hall. Many of the participants on this day took advantage of the view from the hall's loft, which was dismantled soon after the camp opened. (Courtesy of Ele Richardson.)

PROGRAM

Dedication of the Cleveland Girl Scout Camp

West Richfield, Ohio — Sunday, June 20, 1937

—o—

Greetings to the Guests ....Mrs. Stanlee T. Bates
Chairman of Dedication Committee

Transfer of Deed of Property ....Mr. James B. Kirby

Acceptance of Deed of Property ....Mrs. Henry Friede
Commissioner of The Cleveland Girl Scout Council

—o—

Ceremony for Camp Dedication......By Cleveland Girl Scouts

Episodes:

1. Pan and the Wood Nymphs
2. Animal Creatures
3. Fire
4. Water
5. Sky

Instrumental Accompaniment by Akron Girl Scout Pipers

—o—

The entire audience will proceed to the Lodge at the upper end of the Lake for Flag Raising.

Flag Ceremony ....Mrs. Rudolph H. Garfield
Chaimman of Camp Committee

Presentation of Flag Pole ....Mr. John Homer Kapp
President of Civitan Club

Presentation of Flag ....Mrs. W. L. Lamprecht
Moses Cleaveland Chapter, D. A. R.

Girl Scout Color Ceremony ....Girl Scout Troop 57

THE STAR SPANGLED BANNER ....By the audience

—o—

The Scouts hope you will walk about to visit as many units as possible. Refreshments will be served in the units.

The *Plain Dealer* reported that 4,000 people attended the dedication of the camp. Guests were invited to visit the various tent units, where refreshments would be served. (Courtesy of Richfield Historical Society.)

These girls, assigned to the Windy Hill tent unit, were among the first to stay at Camp Julia Crowell in 1937. June Story (first row, second from right) was there under protest. She survived the two-week session and loved it; "As soon as I got home, I was homesick for camp. So my father signed me up for the very last session that summer. And I went back. All by myself. No friends. But I sure made friends!" (Courtesy of June Story Gottschling.)

Each day's activities started with an all-camp flag ceremony outside of the dining hall before breakfast. The Girl Scout Promise would be recited: "On my honor, I will try: To do my duty to God and my country, To help people at all times, To obey the Girl Scout laws." (Courtesy of June Story Gottschling.)

Canoeing was a huge draw for summer camp. Eventually, a special interest "paddler unit" was established where girls developed skills, slept overnight on Lake Linnea in an anchored canoe, and when ready, took canoes on multiday river trips. This 1937 photograph shows where it starts: counselors taking the youngest campers on a gentle paddle through the water lilies. (Courtesy of June Story Gottschling.)

As the session progressed, the girls learned how to handle the canoes independently. They were tested for swimming ability and were assigned color-coded bathing caps: red for beginners and yellow for the more advanced beginners. Being able to swim a certain length earned a girl a green cap, which allowed her to swim to designated parts of the lake. Blue caps were for excellent swimmers. (Courtesy of June Story Gottschling.)

This charming boathouse was located on the northern shore of Lake Jinelle (the lower lake), close to the flagpole terrace. It was built by Jim Kirby, whose real estate agent in 1936 described it as "frame and stone with roofed dock. Two extra-large, especially built rowboats included." This boathouse continued to serve even after the new boathouse was built on Lake Linnea in 1969. The old boathouse was demolished in 1984. This postcard was produced by the Cleveland Girl Scout Council. (Author's collection.)

The building in the back left of this 1938 picture is Garfield Hall. Named for Eleanor Garfield, second commissioner of the Cleveland Girl Scout Council, it is the dance hall that Kirby built on springs that was then repurposed as the camp dining hall. The boathouse is on the right. The pier in the foreground stretches halfway across the lake. (Courtesy of Judy Heiser Heit.)

The waterfront staff was constantly on the move, supervising and teaching swimming and boating. Some of them pose here in a rare moment of calm. The woman on the right is "Carrot." The other two are unidentified. (Courtesy of June Story Gottschling.)

All units had to do a service project for the camp, above and beyond their usual chores. June Story's group made a bench out of a log. She remembers drilling the holes for the legs and helping to sand everything smooth: "Everyone helped. Quite a lovely piece when we got through." In this photograph, the counselors are carrying the completed project to Garfield Hall. (Courtesy of June Story Gottschling.)

The massive stone fireplace of Garfield Hall is just barely visible in the background of this c. 1969 image. Meals were served "family style" after singing grace—a blessing before meals. Girl Scouts learned several graces. It became a tradition at Camp Julia Crowell that singing the "Johnny Appleseed" grace would cause it to rain within 24 hours. (Courtesy of Girl Scouts of North East Ohio.)

At mealtime, everyone had a job. Hoppers brought the plates of food from the kitchen. Hostesses led the singing of grace. Scrapers, washers, and sweepers cleaned up afterward. In this 1960s picture, taken inside Garfield Hall, a sweeper pauses while girls still at the table raise their hands in the quiet sign before listening to announcements or learning a new song. (Courtesy of Girl Scouts of North East Ohio.)

When the tables were cleared, there was dancing. New girls might be warned about the floor, or they might be allowed to find out for themselves what happens when dozens of girls gallop across a spring-loaded dance floor. The girls in this 1988 photograph are spread out across Garfield Hall and appear to be going through the motions of "Queen Mary," a song that features a sailor's hornpipe dance in the chorus. (Courtesy of Girl Scouts of North East Ohio.)

This one-room cabin was built behind Garfield Hall in 1937 so that the resident camp cook could live in it during the summers. The thick shade of the surrounding hemlock trees would help keep the cabin cool in the summer heat. (Courtesy of Girl Scouts of North East Ohio.)

Campers carried cookout supplies for their unit in woven pack baskets. The girl on the right also carries a thermos of cold milk. Katherine "Kinta" Hardon, the camp dietician in 1937, wrote in her journal about the camp kitchen, "The lodge across lake was large enough to house dining hall, kitchens extended beyond lodge—it had spring water which chilled the milk, there was no electricity in kitchen appliances, oven used gas propane burners, we beat all birthday cake by hand, bought fresh milk from Hudson Boys School, private school with its own herd of cows." (Courtesy of June Story Gottschling.)

Counselors at Camp Julia Crowell still wore regulation bloomers, middy blouses, and neckerchiefs in 1937, even though campers wore their regular "civilian" clothes. The counselor at left even has the "official" Girl Scout socks with a trefoil on the cuff. (Courtesy of Girl Scouts of North East Ohio.)

Overnight "Gypsy Hikes" were common in the early days of Girl Scouting. June Story Gottschling remembers, "We were going through farmers' fields and across country lanes. We took a whole day just to get to the barn where we were to sleep at night. Then we hiked back on a different route." The girls took a brief rest break on haystacks they found along the way. (Courtesy of June Story Gottschling.)

"There were no such things as sleeping bags," says June Story Gottschling. "We made bedrolls out of ordinary blankets, and we carried them hanging down on either side of our necks." The girls spread out their bedrolls in the farmer's field and slept under the open sky. Had it rained, they would have been able to sleep in the barn. (Courtesy of June Story Gottschling.)

From the meadow above Lake Linnea, girls could see the Neal House (later named Amity House after Girl Scouts bought the adjoining Neal property). They called it "the Forbidden Castle." Joan Story Gottschling said one of her best memories is when they took their bedrolls to that meadow and watched shooting stars until they fell asleep. She said, "I learned that if I didn't try something, I'd never be able to enjoy it. I learned that at camp because I let go a lot of my fears." (Courtesy of Girl Scouts of North East Ohio.)

A camp counselor's "civilian name" is left behind when at camp. She can only be known by her camp identity. The 1937 summer camp staff in this portrait were identified as, from left to right, (first row) Phoebe, Penny, Buddy, and Nicky; (second row) Dinkle, Jala, Wee-Soo, Sola, Robin, Tuck, Tim, Pixie, and Eliska; (third row) March, Splash, Meta, unidentified, Sandy, Jerry, Bill, Russe, Piper, Kinta, and Downy. (Courtesy of Girl Scouts of North East Ohio.)

From left to right, Georgiana Morris, Janet Flinn, Dorothy Mallory (standing), Virginia Wilson, Billy Ann Lidyard, Rae Ochsner, Jeanne Potts, and Ann Hoop fire up their voices as they sing in front of the Garfield Hall fireplace in December 1937. (Photograph from the *Cleveland Press*; courtesy of Special Collections, Michael Schwartz Library, Cleveland State University.)

Heavy icicles at the entrance to the swinging bridge were formed by the spray off the dam spillway around 1940. Troops were encouraged to visit camp during the winter. The farmer/camp manager would regularly test the ice and telephone a report to the council office from anyone inquiring about ice-skating. (Courtesy of Girl Scouts of North East Ohio.)

Henry Heiser, the tenant farmer/camp manager, pauses to look out over Lake Jinelle in May 1938. The intersect drain in the center of the lake has a small island around it. (Courtesy of Judy Heiser Heit.)

Girls slept and stored their gear in tents, but they mostly lived outside. Here, a group is gathered at the edge of a tent in the Orchard Way unit in July 1940. (Photograph by Byron Filkins for the *Cleveland Press*; courtesy of Special Collections, Michael Schwartz Library, Cleveland State University.)

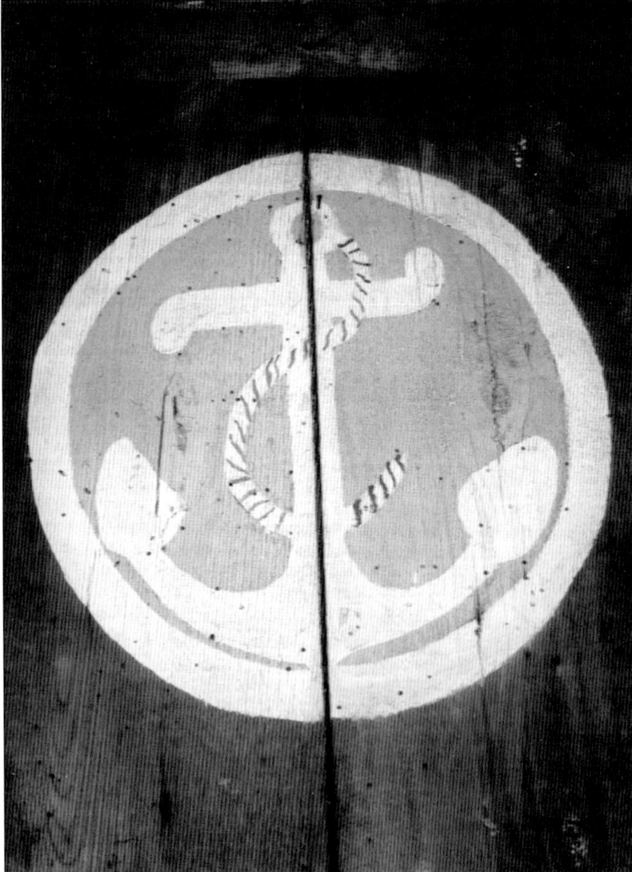

When it was built in 1940, Seely Cabin was deep in the woods, far removed from the only camp entrance, which was back on Oviatt Road at State Route 303. Seely served as a place for campers focused on boating skills. Funding for the little cabin was donated by Warner and Emma Seely. Warner had served as chair of the Camp Solicitation Committee, and Emma was the third commissioner of the Cleveland Girl Scout Council. (Courtesy of Rob Richardson.)

Seely Cabin was built of wormy chestnut wood. Girl Scout artists painted this boating badge above the fieldstone fireplace. The lifesaver badge and swimming badge were painted on either side. The window sills were decorated with stenciled sailboats, anchors, and buoys. (Courtesy of Rob Richardson.)

From this sketch map of the camp from 1964, one can get a sense of how isolated Seely Cabin was prior to the purchase of the Neal property. The road to Hilaka in the upper left did not yet exist. The main road in camp curved on the left (west) side of Lake Jinelle (the lower lake). In front of Garfield Hall, the road curved up toward Fernwood before fading out. From there, the trail toward Seely was a long upward trek. (Map by Lake Erie Girl Scout Council; courtesy of Sherry Patkovsec.)

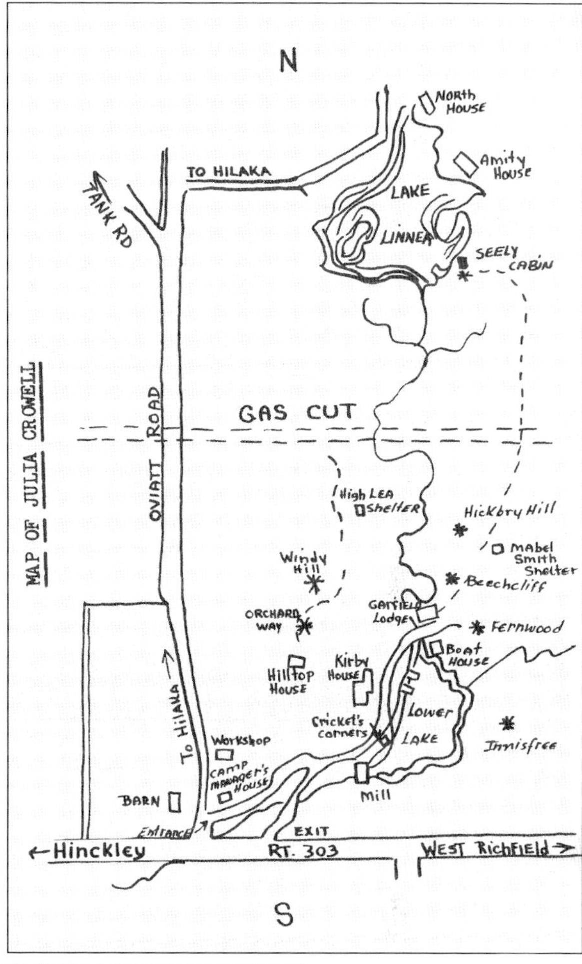

Senior Scouts gather around the outdoor fireplace of Seely Cabin in May 1949 to make "Porcupine Joes." Pictured are Ginny Moorehead, Sal Howe, Carol Birchmeier, Prudy Hesche, and Doris Rogens. (Photograph from the *Cleveland Press*; courtesy of Special Collections, Michael Schwartz Library, Cleveland State University.)

Riolama Shaw, Marjorie Mogge, Missy Icove, and Mary Allen wash up on July 16, 1941. Girls had to pump their own water and carry it to where it was needed. (Photograph by Brian Filkins for the *Cleveland Press*; courtesy of Special Collections, Michael Schwartz Library, Cleveland State University.)

Counselors Doris Ludaster and Anne Stanges supervise the popular archery practice in an open field. Campers Janet Sweeney, Suzanne Phillips, and Betsy Ann Jones take aim on July 16, 1941. (Photograph by Brian Filkins for the *Cleveland Press*; courtesy of Special Collections, Michael Schwartz Library, Cleveland State University.)

Katherine Winsiger, Shirley Fike, Myra Glasser, and Katheryn Hanna are getting ready to set sail in July 1942. World War II was on the photographer's mind as he wrote on the back, "No U Boats here." (Photograph by Walter Kneale for the *Cleveland Press*; courtesy of Special Collections, Michael Schwartz Library, Cleveland State University.)

Betsy Hauserm, Carol Hanson, Janet Lauster, and Alice Campbell sketch near the waterwheel of Kirby's Mill on July 13, 1942. When the Girl Scouts bought the Kirby estate in 1937, the mill was converted into the arts and crafts studio. Its unique appeal was also an artistic inspiration for many to this day. (Photograph by Walter Kneale for the *Cleveland Press*; courtesy of Special Collections, Michael Schwartz Library, Cleveland State University.)

A 1937 article in the *Cleveland Plain Dealer* noted that Brownies at the Orchard Way tent unit went through "the ceremony of having magic powder blown on them so that they can ascend to 'Wendy's House' at the edge of 'Never, Never Land.' Wendy's House is a tree house built especially for Brownie tea parties and story hours." The article went on to say that "girls from Orchard Way will follow a paper trail to the upper lake. They will dress in masquerade costumes depicting their favorite imaginative characters." Although the *Press* photographer labeled this image "Brownie Nest," it was likely the same as Wendy's House. Located in the "backyard" of Hilltop House, this photograph actually predated the cabin's construction. Jane Lowell, Janet Sloan, Lois Williams, and Karyl Hale perch in the tree while Harriet Newhaus and Ruth Nemrow negotiate the ladder in July 1942. (Photograph by Walter Kneale for the *Cleveland Press*; courtesy of Special Collections, Michael Schwartz Library, Cleveland State University.)

Lucia Howarth, Gwendolyn Gregory, Jacqueline Spencer, Ellen Hofmann, and Doris Burgett prepare their meal in a Dutch oven in 1942. Although girls ate most meals in the dining hall, cooking out at their tent unit was part of most programs. Summer camp brochures from the 1940s spelled out that Camp Julia Crowell admitted all girls, regardless of race. (Photograph by Walter Kneale for the *Cleveland Press*; courtesy of Special Collections, Michael Schwartz Library, Cleveland State University.)

Hilltop House was built in 1950 as an additional winterized cabin. But the Cleveland Girl Scout Council knew it would not be enough. A capital campaign was launched to expand and improve campsites and purchase land for a second camp. By 1954, the council was able to open Camp Margaret Bates in Macedonia, but there was no more money left over for Camp Julia Crowell. (Courtesy of Girl Scouts of North East Ohio.)

Hilltop House was a single-room cabin. Its location above Kirby's old orchard gave it a magnificent view of the wooded valley below. In its backyard was an old tree with a platform treehouse for Brownies. (Courtesy of Girl Scouts of North East Ohio.)

Sleeping arrangements at Hilltop House included Murphy beds that folded into the walls. It featured both an indoor bathroom and an outhouse. (Courtesy of Girl Scouts of North East Ohio.)

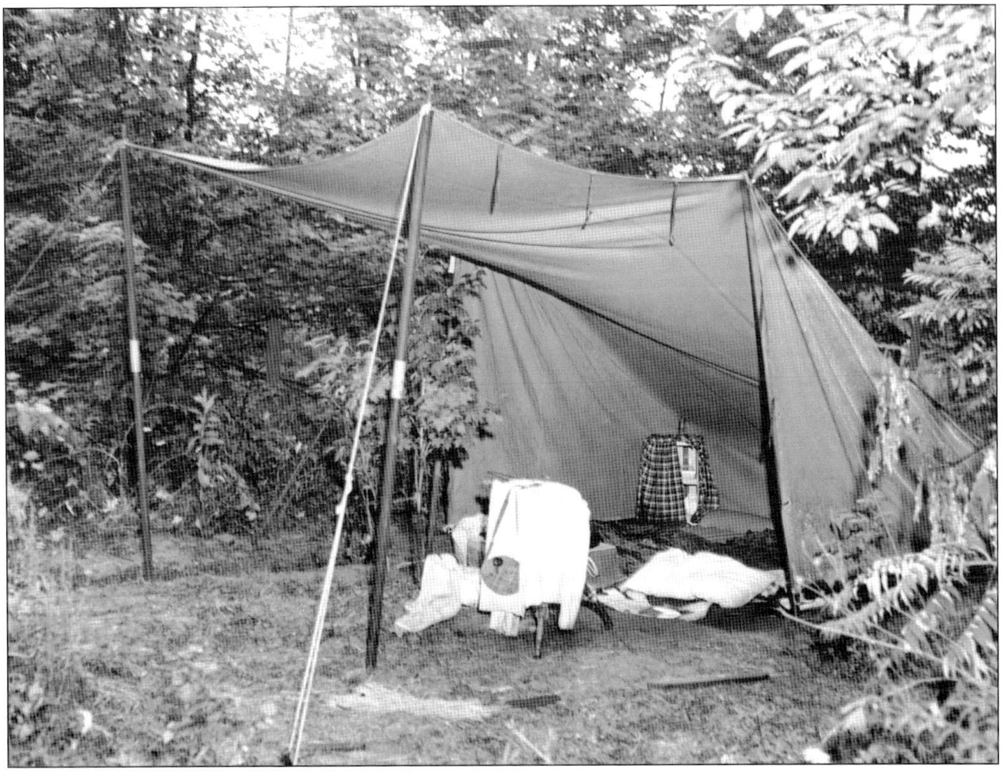

Sallie Parker of Cleveland Heights and June Gamble of Pittsburgh, both age 13, were sleeping in a "baker's tent" like this when they were killed during a lightning storm in the wee hours of the morning of August 4, 1959. Two other girls were injured but survived. (Photograph from the *Cleveland Press*; courtesy of Special Collections, Michael Schwartz Library, Cleveland State University.)

GIRL SCOUT SALLY PARKER was killed by light-

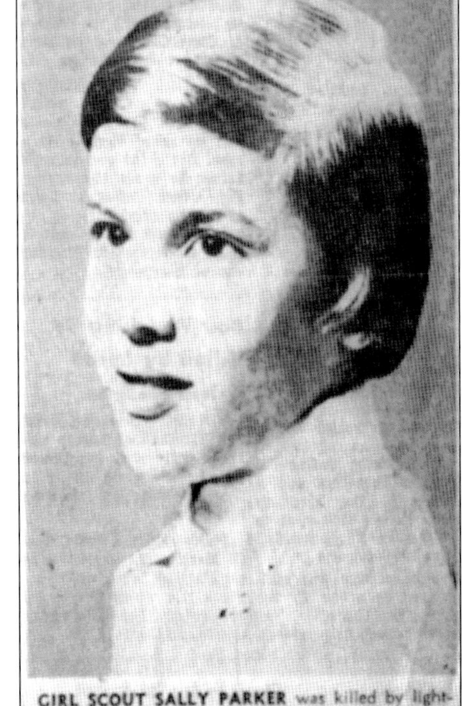

June Gamble and Sallie Parker's deaths stunned the camp and the entire community, but the camp continued on. A few girls were pulled out, but most stayed. (Photograph from the *Cleveland Press*; courtesy of Girl Scouts of North East Ohio.)

The A-frame High Lea Shelter (above, left) was built as a memorial to Sallie Parker. Her family contributed the companion hexagonal outdoor kitchen several years later (above, right). Until the shelter was built, the area had been called Skanawunde Meadow, or "Skanny" for short. But High Lea became the preferred name. (Left, courtesy of Girl Scouts of North East Ohio; right, courtesy of Rob Richardson.)

The meadow across from Hickory Hill unit had long been a place for all-camp gatherings. This shelter designed by Mable Smith and constructed as a memorial to her made the site more versatile. (Courtesy of Debbie Kramer.)

First aid is an important skill learned by Girl Scouts. Here, Doris Hiebsch and Marion Geiger get out their first aid kit for a baby bunny they found at camp, a practice no longer recommended. (Photograph by Fred Bottomer for the *Cleveland Press*; courtesy of Special Collections, Michael Schwartz Library, Cleveland State University.)

The mill meadow was a picturesque spot for games in summer, as seen in this 1959 photograph. The embankment of the dam made it a gentle sledding hill in winter. (Photograph by John Nash for the *Cleveland Press*; courtesy of Special Collections, Michael Schwartz Library, Cleveland State University.)

The Forest of the Lost Green Cathedral began as a way to earn funds to support the camp. Rows of pines were planted as a Christmas tree farm near the new Hilaka entrance off Oviatt Road. As the trees grew taller, the arching canopy reminded some of a cathedral. An open-air chapel was constructed—and then mysteriously vanished without a trace. Only the name remains in the place where it may have been. This 1960 photograph shows Christmas tree shoppers, Mrs. Harry Caldwell (center) and her daughters Karen (left) and Charlene (right). (Courtesy of Girl Scouts of North East Ohio.)

This first day cover from the Girl Scouts' 1962 National Senior Roundup in Button Bay, Vermont, featured Kirby's Mill and commemorated the silver anniversary of Camp Julia Crowell. National Senior Roundups were held every three years. (Author's collection.)

Five

NEAL FRUIT FARM

The northern third of Richfield Heritage Preserve was once part of an extensive farm owned by Nathaniel Oviatt, brother to Heman Oviatt and one of the first Richfield Township trustees. When Nathaniel's daughter Ruth married Milton R. Freeman in 1856, Nathaniel allocated his holdings west of Broadview Road to the couple while still retaining legal ownership of the land.

Ruth's diary of 1862 recorded that she and Milton had two little girls: Hattie, age four, and Emma, age two. That year, Ruth's two brothers, John and Charles, died while serving in the Union army. Milton went to Kentucky to bring John's body home and caught typhoid. The girls had measles. Ruth had measles and diphtheria. Even so, she barely stopped her cooking, cleaning, sewing, and chores. She volunteered at church and took care of her father in his house across the street. She visited with family and friends, harvested the garden, and made and sold butter. She was with her sister Sarah as she died. At the end of the year, Ruth, indomitable and resolute, wrote, "I have today been taking a view of my life during the year and feel that I have great reasons to thank and praise my Heavenly Father for his goodness and mercy to me. Although He has seen fit to take from me two precious brothers and a darling sister . . . yet I will praise God."

In 1918, the Neal family purchased the Oviatt/Freeman farm and started an orchard as a hobby. Their main business was the Cleveland-based Neal Moving and Storage Company. Clarence Neal grew to love his apple trees and the apple business, building a roadside market and a cider-processing plant on the site of the old Freeman farm buildings. Herbert Neal inherited the businesses and worked to modernize the operation. Labor shortages during World War II and the pressures of running two disparate businesses led Herbert to scale back and sell off acreage. But it was a final crop failure in the mid-1950s that forced the Neals to sell the last remnant of their orchard to the Girl Scouts and leave Richfield.

The prosperous Oviatt/Freeman farm is pictured above in an etching from the 1874 Summit County Atlas. The gate posts were later repurposed in the Amity House outdoor fireplace. Building material from the Oviatt/Freeman farm structures was incorporated into the Neals' roadside stand around 1930 and was retained in the Country Counter Market and the current Giant Eagle grocery store. (Courtesy of Akron-Summit County Public Library.)

In 1918, Clarence "C.J." Neal (right) is pictured on his hungry horse, Indian, in the backyard of his country house, the old Freeman farmhouse on Broadview Road. William (left) and Herbert (center) Neal stand on the cart with their pony, Regret. Within two years, C.J. turned from general farming to the cultivation of apple trees. (Courtesy of the Herbert C. Neal family.)

C.J. Neal trained to be a lawyer but practiced for only a short while before becoming president of the Neal Moving and Storage Company. He also accepted some political assignments. The clipping at right celebrates Neal's appointment to the Cleveland school board while still the young father of two little boys. (Photograph from the *Cleveland Press*; courtesy of Special Collections, Michael Schwartz Library, Cleveland State University.)

In 1924, the Neals' neighbor Jim Kirby approached them with an offer to create a lake on their southern boundary. As the valley became a lake, the Neals decided to build a weekend cottage overlooking the water. This photograph shows the Neals' house when it was new, with a sweeping circular drive. Steps lead up to a stone terrace and the front door. (Courtesy of the Herbert C. Neal family.)

Bricks to construct the Neals' home came from the demolition of buildings on Cleveland's Public Square. The buildings pictured above were on the southwest corner of the square in 1922, shortly before they were torn down to make room for the Union Terminal Tower. The used bricks were carried down to Richfield in the Neal moving vans. (Courtesy of Cleveland Public Library Photograph Collection.)

Just across the driveway from the house was a three-car garage with living quarters for the groundskeeper upstairs. After the Girl Scouts acquired the property, the bay doors were bricked in. The structure became a popular camping cabin, appropriately named Coach House. (Courtesy of the Herbert C. Neal family.)

In this undated photograph, the family dog, Pete, peeks through the archway of the Neals' side door. An edge of the gardens and the gables of the garage are visible behind him. The arch no longer exists but was pictured as late as 1964 in an insurance photograph. (Courtesy of the Herbert C. Neal family.)

The Neal family relaxes on the terrace of their new house (later known as North House) overlooking the lake. Clarence Neal is in the center in a tie. William is on the left holding Pete. Herbert and Clara are seated in the back on the wall. (Courtesy of the Herbert C. Neal family.)

The view from the terrace of the Neals' house in 1945 includes a favorite stone lantern in the foreground. The Neals traveled the world, bringing back exotic souvenirs to decorate their home in Richfield. (Courtesy of the Herbert C. Neal family.)

The interior of the Neals' house appears sparse after the family moved on and the Girl Scouts moved in. But generations of campers appreciated the reflections of its former grandeur, such as the massive vaulted ceiling and the painting of the ship embedded over the fireplace. (Courtesy of Rob Richardson.)

At about the time the Neals finished their new house in 1928, their first apple trees were mature enough to bear fruit. They converted the old Oviatt/Freeman farm complex on Broadview Road into a roadside fruit stand and cider-processing plant. (Courtesy of the Herbert C. Neal family.)

The Neals advertised the fruit farm heavily in Cleveland. City families going for a ride in the county would pull their cars into the unpaved parking lot of the Neal Fruit Farm showroom on Broadview Road. (Courtesy of the Herbert C. Neal family.)

William (left) and Herbert (right) Neal pose with their cross-country skis on the cobblestone dam. The Neal family maintained their primary residence on Detroit Road in Cleveland, coming down to the farm on weekends and holidays. (Courtesy of the Herbert C. Neal family.)

In 1945, when Herbert Neal took this picture, the dam of the Neals' irrigation pond was composed of cobblestones. An undated photograph in the Kirby album at the Richfield Historical Society shows a new concrete face on the center of this dam, suggesting that Jim Kirby may have assisted the Neals with the dam repair after he had moved away. (Courtesy of the Herbert C. Neal family.)

When the Neals' older son Herbert married Helen Pocock in 1934, his parents built Amity House for them as a wedding gift. It became Herbert and Helen's primary home. Lake Linnea is visible in the background as the house rises on its eastern shore. (Courtesy of the Herbert C. Neal family.)

When Amity House construction was complete, awnings and a valance added finishing touches. The lawn sloped gently down to Lake Linnea. (Courtesy of the Herbert C. Neal family.)

Amity House was constructed in the French Normandy style, characterized by a tower with a conical roof, reminiscent of medieval French farmhouses with attached silos. A unique weather vane on the Amity House turret is one of many charming details. (Courtesy of Rob Richardson.)

In November 1936, Helen Pocock Neal gave birth to a daughter, Barbara. Helen and baby Barbara are flanked by Helen's grandmother Addie Richards (left) and mother Grace Pocock (right) in the living room of Amity House. (Courtesy of the Herbert C. Neal family.)

The day before Barbara Neal was born, her grandfather Clarence was out inspecting the orchard when he had a massive heart attack. His body was found under one of his beloved apple trees. He was only 57 years old. Clarence's death threw the responsibility of the Neal businesses onto Herbert. (Courtesy of the Herbert C. Neal family.)

Amity House is in the center of this undated aerial view of Lake Linnea. Clara Neal once declared that if her husband could plant thousands of apple trees, then she could plant thousands of pines to remind her of Germany's Black Forest. Her pines and spruces lined the western shore of the lake and the valley to the north. (Courtesy of Richfield Historical Society.)

A clay tennis court was installed between the two Neal houses. Stone steps in the foreground led downslope to the head of Lake Linnea. (Courtesy of the Herbert C. Neal family.)

These visitors parked briefly in front of Amity House as they head toward the driveway on the opposite of the house from where it is now. Note the screening on the side porch. (Courtesy of the Herbert C. Neal family.)

Herbert Neal and his daughter Barbara prepare to go fishing in their lake. The brick walkway at their feet was adjacent to the side porch of their home (later named Amity House). The Neals' clay tennis court is visible in the background. Barbara recalls that there was a fire hydrant near the tennis court, and that her father would hook up a fire hose to spray water on bats roosting under the porch roof to discourage then from settling there. (Courtesy of the Herbert C. Neal family.)

Bill Neal relaxes in his boat on Lake Linnea. Neal recorded his recollections on audiotape, which was transcribed by his niece Barbara, who maintained the family history archive. (Courtesy of the Herbert C. Neal family.)

Barbara Neal's little sister Janet was born in 1938. A few years later, the girls ride their bikes together on the double-curved driveway between Amity House and their grandmother's house on the other side of the creek. (Courtesy of the Herbert C. Neal family.)

Barbara and Janet Neal look tiny as they huddle together on the southeast porch of Amity House. This photograph was taken by their father in 1945. The ivy that would eventually cover the house is just beginning to cover the brickwork. (Courtesy of the Herbert C. Neal family.)

The Neals enjoyed the lake they shared with the Girl Scouts. In this 1945 image, Janet Neal wades while Barbara and their cousin Martha dangle their feet off the dock and cousin Linda stands watching. Mary Alice, the wife of Bill Neal and mother of Martha and Linda, faces away from the camera. (Courtesy of the Herbert C. Neal family.)

Herbert Neal inspects produce in the Neal Fruit Farm showroom. Neal began downsizing the orchards after World War II when it became harder to find harvest workers. The cider plant and showroom were later sold to Ralph Vaughn, who turned them into the County Counter grocery store. Crop failure in the mid-1950s was the final blow. The Neals had to sell their remaining land. (Courtesy of the Herbert C. Neal family.)

Six

Hilaka

In 1957, purchase of the land that became Camp Hilaka was hugely controversial.

Only three years prior, the Cleveland Girl Scout Council held a fundraising campaign for camp expansion. They raised enough money to buy land for a new camp in Macedonia, which they named Camp Margaret Bates. But they had not brought in enough funds for planned new facilities at Camp Julia Crowell. Then without warning, the Neal family offered to sell their land to the Scouts. With all their financial resources tapped out, some in the council said that they could not afford to buy more land. Others pointed out that they could not afford not to buy it. If a new owner decided to dump industrial waste or raw sewage into Lake Linnea, the pollution would flow directly down into the lower lake, destroying the swimming and boating there. In the end, the council decided to risk becoming overextended. It bought the 93-acre Neal property to add to Camp Julia Crowell.

The graceful houses that came with the land inspired a new vision of the property—this was no longer an ordinary camp. It had the potential to become a regional or even an international destination. With a feeling that the new part of the property required new branding, the council coined the name "Hilaka" to honor the upper lake. A new entrance directly into Hilaka was created off the upper part of Oviatt Road. The focus of the combined camps shifted with the addition of a new central dining hall and another new entrance from Broadview Road. Upgrades and additions continued even as the social upheaval of the 1960s and 1970s was about to change how girls thought of camp.

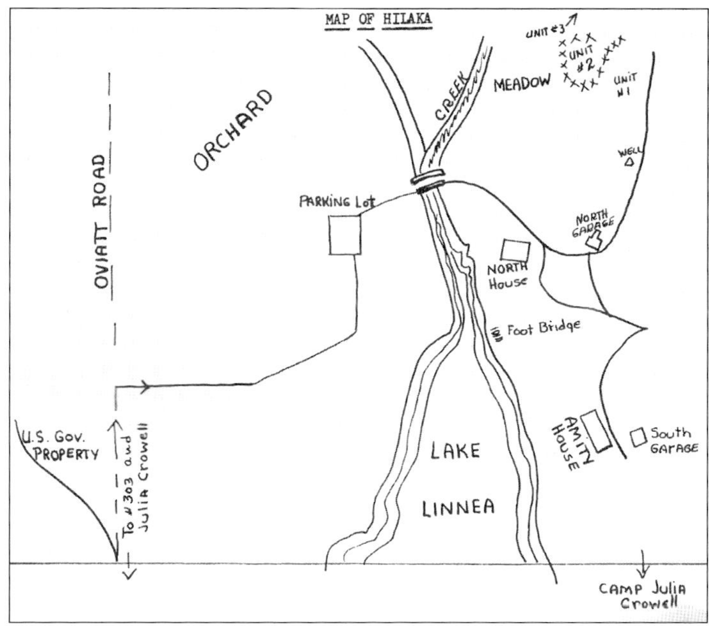

In this sketch map printed in the council's official camp guide from 1964, Hilaka is identified only as the part of the camp purchased from the Neals. Eventually, the gas cut became the generally accepted boundary, and everything north of it was considered as "the Hilaka side." The camp entrance was on Oviatt Road just north of the road to "U.S. Gov. Property"—the tank testing grounds. (Map by Lake Erie Girl Scout Council; courtesy of Sherry Petkovsec.)

This picture was taken in the living room of Amity House at Hilaka. The back of this is labeled "Co-ed weekend at Julia Crowell, 1961," reflecting the ambiguity of the camp name, which lasted several years. Amity was first used as an "adults only" or special events space. (Courtesy of Sherry Petkovsek.)

The Amity basement was a game room that doubled as a storm shelter. Although leaders worried about the dangers of severe weather, girls were sometimes known to enjoy the excitement of being evacuated to one of the house basements during tornadoes. In these situations, the counselors were trained to keep the atmosphere light with games and songs. This photograph is from 1988. (Courtesy of Girl Scouts of North East Ohio.)

The masthead for the council's newsletter, the *Millwheel*, was redrawn in 1963 by Cleveland artist and Girl Scout mom Grace Spears. The *Millwheel* had served as the Cleveland Girl Scout Council newsletter since at least 1952. It continued after Cleveland merged with the Lake and Geauga County Councils to become Lake Erie Girl Scout Council. (Courtesy of Girl Scouts of North East Ohio.)

Howard E. Holmes, manager of the Chevrolet plant in Brook Park, presents a check for $15,000 for the camp fund to Cadette Scout Marilyn Duffey while Junior Scout Molly Donly and Senior Scout Rozelle Hill look on. The capital campaign took place during the nationally mandated council merger. (Courtesy of Special Collections, Michael Schwartz Library, Cleveland State University.)

The new dining hall, named for George Gund, was opened in time for the 1967 summer resident camp season. Indoor restrooms were not added until the 1990s. (Courtesy of Girl Scouts of North East Ohio.)

The kitchen of Gund Hall was fully equipped with up-to-date, industrial-strength appliances. Large windows let in plenty of natural light, unlike the hastily built kitchen at Garfield. There was storage and counter space that had been previously unimaginable. (Courtesy of Girl Scouts of North East Ohio.)

The spacious interior of Gund Hall meant that everyone attending resident camp could eat at the same time. Mealtimes were followed by clean up and then all-camp singalongs. (Courtesy of Girl Scouts of North East Ohio.)

Hand in Hand with Community

Our Camps Widen Horizons

The Louis D. Beaumont swimming pool opened in 1967, just a few hours before the summer camp staff arrived. This clipping from the council's newsletter, the *Millwheel*, describes how the expanded facilities at Crowell Hilaka allowed the council to bring in 160 inner-city girls to resident camp. (Courtesy of Girl Scouts of North East Ohio.)

From the gas cut, hikers could easily reach the open field along the western boundary. Just on the other side of the fence were the tank testing grounds. Girls could watch the tanks rolling by or, at night, catch glimpses of their headlights through the trees. The roaring of the tanks long into the night was a memorable feature of camp through the 1960s. (Courtesy of Christine Stark.)

Girl Scouts were famous for the invention of s'mores: toasted marshmallow with chocolate bars smooshed between graham crackers. The girls here were cooking a much more substantial meal in their campsite on the gas cut in 1966. They learned to devise one-pot meals, plank fish and steak, and bake in reflector ovens and in bean holes. (Courtesy of Christine Stark.)

The Wonken Tonken tent unit opened in 1967. It was originally named Waken Tonka by the counselors in training (CITs) who lived there that summer. The name came from the Lakota phrase meaning "great spirit" and was inspired by a storyteller from the Ojibway tribe who had met many of the girls during a canoe trip the previous summer. (Courtesy of Rob Richardson.)

With a new swimming pool and shower house and a new dining hall connected by a new driveway to the new entrance on Broadview Road, Crowell Hilaka was ready to unveil its glories for the world by hosting a National Senior Roundup in 1968. Normally held every three years, GSUSA decided to hold only regional events in 1968. Senior Scouts (high school age) from 40 different states attended as well as 18 Girl Guides from Canada. Five poles were erected at Gund Hall to fly the flags of the United States, Canada, Columbia, Cypress, and the World Association of Girl Guides and Girl Scouts. Memorable moments of the event included an evening at Blossom Music Center and a trip to General Electric to witness an amazing new invention—the microwave oven. Here, senior girls attending the roundup learn about Kirby's Mill. (Courtesy of Girl Scouts of North East Ohio.)

The final structures to be built with funds from the 1963 capital campaign were the new boathouse and dock on Lake Linnea. The boathouse roof was used for sleeping under the stars on hot summer nights. (Courtesy of Girl Scouts of North East Ohio.)

Camp alumna Laurel Freeder remembers, "They were very protective about the many beautiful water lilies that Mr. Kirby imported. There was a $10 fine if you were caught picking one! They had a scent, and we would carefully sniff as we rowed by them. One time, I sunk one. I caught it with my paddle from underneath, and it went right down. I was terrified! My parents would have KILLED me if I had a $10 fine! We rowed away so fast." (Courtesy of Rob Richardson.)

Camp alumna Laurel Freeder continues her story. "One memorable (and scary!) time, I almost went over the dam in a boat. Not intentionally. We were looking straight down the drop. Holy crap, we're going over! Row for your life! We weren't supposed to have gotten that close. Another rule." (Courtesy of Girl Scouts of North East Ohio.)

In 1967, the Chagrin Valley Association, composed of Girl Scout service units in southeastern Cuyahoga County, donated the funds to construct Chagrin Valley Cabin. In 1969, the Rotary Club contributed the funds to build a duplicate cabin, which was named Gemini, pictured here. (Courtesy of Rob Richardson.)

In 1974, plans to widen State Route 303 posed a potential threat to Kirby's Mill. The council responded by applying to place the mill in the National Register of Historic Places. The process took five years. During that time, council volunteers Georgianna Bonds and Nan Prior led the effort to turn the mill into a museum of Girl Scout history. (Courtesy of Girl Scouts of North East Ohio.)

In 1976, Kirby's boat launch/picnic shelter (left) was dedicated in honor of the council's bicentennial "Hidden Heroine," Helen Peterjohn (right), whose camp name was Cricket. Camp alumna Patricia Prinkey wrote about Cricket's Corner, "Once you go down the steps it is like another world down there. People on the road above have no idea you are below." (Left, courtesy of Rob Richardson; right, courtesy of Girl Scouts of North East Ohio.)

The site of the Far Away Pines tent unit (shown here in 1980) was once part of the Neals' apple orchard, as was all of Hilaka. What was unusual about this particular meadow is that it is almost encircled by tall evergreens. These were planted by Clara Neal in the 1920s and 1930s to outline the rim of the many creek valleys that ran through the orchards. (Courtesy of Girl Scouts of North East Ohio.)

Operation Broomstick was the name given to the springtime efforts to get the camp ready for warm weather and resident camp. Tents were raised, cots and mattresses were hauled out of winter storage, and general sprucing up commenced. Adult volunteers, families, Cadette and Senior troops, and even Boy Scout troops were recruited to help (Courtesy of Girl Scouts of North East Ohio.)

SOHIO "GIVES A DAM"

Council executive director Arlene Tobias (left) and council president Georgianna Bonds (right) present an appropriate T-shirt to John R. Miller, president of the Standard Oil Company (Sohio). Sohio had made a substantial contribution toward repairs on the two major dams of Crowell Hilaka in 1981. (Courtesy of Girl Scouts of North East Ohio.)

Here, the spillway of Lake Jinelle's dam receives an upgrade in 1980. Twenty-five years later, state flood-control regulations became stricter, and the lower dam was no longer in compliance. This may have been a contributing factor in the council's decision to sell Crowell Hilaka. The problem was solved in 2019 by the Richfield Joint Recreation District. (Courtesy of Girl Scouts of North East Ohio.)

In 1984, the council built the open-sided summer barn in response to members' request for horseback riding programs at camp. At first, horses were leased for the summer. In 1992, the council purchased horses, built the winter barn, and offered year-round horse programing. Even girls who were not riding enjoyed going to the barn or the pastures to visit the horses. (Courtesy of Dawn Woodward.)

In 1992, the council built the winter barn and bought their own horses. Lessons and trail rides were offered year-round. Here, Erica Smith enjoys her first horseback ride. (Author's collection.)

Spif (Lisa Lee Pruett) was a very active Girl Scout, counselor in training, and Gold Award recipient who was tragically killed. The dedication of Spif's Garden took place on June 1, 1991. Located just north of Amity House on the site of the Neals' clay tennis court, it became a shady place for contemplation and quiet conversation. (Courtesy of Debbie Kramer.)

Stan Polo, the last manager of Crowell Hilaka, found the rock for Spif's memorial in one of the camp creeks and moved it up to the garden. Spif's troop and family return annually to tend the garden. (Courtesy of Rob Richardson.)

Campers scale the heights of the high-ropes challenge course (left). The course was added to Crowell Hilaka in 1995. It was one of the first such courses in northeast Ohio. Camp director Beasley (Debbie Kramer) tried out the zip line herself before going on to become a facilitator for the high-ropes course (right). Participants said that the course helped them conquer fear and build confidence. (Both, courtesy of Debbie Kramer.)

The challenge courses were located deep in the woods between Mable Smith Meadow and Fernwood Shelter. Here, from left to right, resident camp counselors Juniper, Yakko, Timber, and Dopey take a break on an element of the low-ropes challenge course. (Courtesy of Dawn Woodward.)

Seven

Camp Life

Resident camp took place in the summer. Initially, a single session of resident camp lasted for two weeks. Later, it was reduced to one week. Girls registered individually, meaning they might not know anyone else at camp.

Troop camping, a weekend at camp, could take place any time during the year. Theoretically, the girls—not the adults—plan the events, menus, and responsibilities for the weekend. Variations on troop camping included core camp, initiated in 1988, where program staff would provide some of the activities for an inexperienced troop. In service unit camporees, all the troops in a defined area plan a weekend camp event, often with a theme.

Crowell Hilaka was a realm apart from a girl's life at home and school.

Summer camp director Mary Hoyes reflected that "camping is more than living outdoors; more than merry quips; singing; hiking; swimming; fishing; listening to nature whisper, rustle, shriek and whistle plus all the other exciting and interesting things that we do. Friendship is our great common denominator. Friends from another school, another part of our council, of another race or religion, of a different age and background, have enlarged our world, have helped us give and take and care for others. Friendship has lightened the camp-keeping chores, taught us to play fair and have fun, given us many happy memories and feel a kinship for all of God's creation."

From left to right, resident camp counselors Star, Shamrock, and Scooby stand ready to welcome campers in 1998. Camp counselors lived in the tent units and were mentors, cheerleaders, and confidants for the girls in their units. Some had camp experience; others did not and learned on the job. (Courtesy of Dawn Woodward.)

For camporees and other special events, long-serving volunteers, affectionately known as "Greenbloods," passed on traditions and knowledge to younger troop leaders. Here, Joyce Randall models her "glory jacket," a hat full of "swaps," and a calm smile during the Bedford service unit camporee of 1995. The event was shifted to Camp Julia Crowell when Camp Margaret Bates was suddenly shut down after an environmental disaster. (Courtesy of Rob Richardson.)

Laura Kirby arrives at resident camp in 1958 with her required gear: a suitcase with clothes and gear for two weeks; an orange crate containing extra gear, which would be used as a bedside stand in the platform tent; and a bedroll. The wagon was supplied by the camp so girls could carry their gear to their assigned tent unit. (Courtesy of Laura Kirby Cronin.)

Each platform tent held four cots. The sides of the tent could be rolled up, which allowed for easy conversation between girls in different tents. Laura Kirby wrote to her parents, "My teddy bear is being used as a note passer. We write a note and tie it to him and throw him over to tent three. They read it, write us a note, and send him back to us again. We keep on doing this until rest period is over. P.S. I don't miss you. So happy you're not here." (Courtesy of Laura Kirby Cronin.)

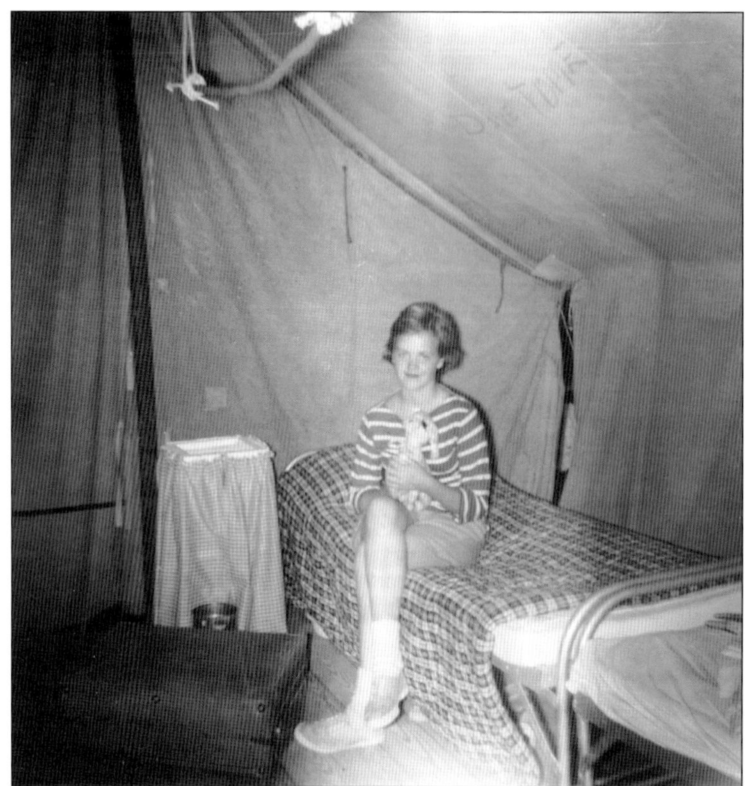

Patricia "Pat" Stevens Robertson sits on her friend Sandy's bed inside a typical platform tent in 1958. Pat's bedside orange crate was fetchingly trimmed with gingham fabric. A tin can vagabond stove is visible inside the crate, and a clothes rack made from a stick is suspended from the tent's ridgepole. (Courtesy of Sandy Scherrer Norris.)

Patricia Stevens Robertson demonstrates personal hygiene at the unit sink. Photographs of tent units from the 1950s do not show shelters. By the 1980s, shelters were a standard part of platform tent sites. (Courtesy of Sandy Scherrer Norris.)

The mill was the craft studio until 1976, but crafts could be made anywhere. Above, from left to right, Twila Winters, Nancy Fleming, and Susan Hengesbach perch on the dam wall to work on projects just outside the studio where they can be close to supplies. At right, Martha Ginn (standing) and Pamela Perry (seated) take their basket weaving supplies back to their unit to work on during free time in 1962. (Both, courtesy of Girl Scouts of North East Ohio.)

"We went on all kinds of hikes in the woods both long and short," says Laurel Freeder about the time she spent at resident camp in the mid-1960s. "I was very proud for many years that I had gone on a ten-mile hike and that I was able to finish it . . . even if I had to sit down for a while! Looking at a map of the camp later, I can see that we weren't that far in the wilderness. But to me, it felt like being dropped into the Amazon. I had no idea were only a few miles from "civilization." . . . It toughened me up and made me confident!" Favorite single-day hike destinations from Crowell Hilaka were Whipps Ledges, Walnut Pony Farm, East Richfield cemetery (where the children of John Brown are buried), and the ice-cream counter in the drugstore at the corner of Broadview Road and State Route 303. (Courtesy of Girl Scouts of North East Ohio.)

"Only one at a time on the bridge" read the sign posted on the mill at the entrance to the swinging bridge. It added to the thrill of danger and excitement as the bridge bounced and swayed next to the water rushing over the spillway. Camp alumna Loise Pilz remembers that crossing the bridge was a test of courage. This photograph was taken in 1977. (Courtesy of Girl Scouts of North East Ohio.)

These young campers learned how to hand off an ax safely. Camp alumna Laurel Freeder enthused, "I loved the idea of 'Being Prepared!' I had a real Girl Scout knife. That was very empowering. It made me feel like, 'I can fight off wild animals, man! I can cut wood for a fire! I am a badass!' " (Courtesy of Girl Scouts of North East Ohio.)

When this outhouse near the old Orchard Way site was dismantled, camp manager Jim Brigham decided to recycle the painted boards into a shelter near the lower lake. He asked one of the summer camp counselors if he should reassemble the images correctly or at random. She told him to mix it up; the resulting shelter appeared to be a work of abstract art. (Courtesy of Girl Scouts of North East Ohio.)

From left to right, Amy Wancheck, Cassandra Sudberry, and Beverly Fuetz use improvised rods to go fishing at the Lake Jinelle dam in July 1963. Kirby House is faintly visible in the background. (Photograph by Frank Reed for the *Cleveland Press*; courtesy of Special Collections, Michael Schwartz Library, Cleveland State University.)

After meals, the counselors or CITs led singalongs. Here, girls gather by the Gund Hall fireplace to consider their next performance piece. Camper Beth Storey reflects, "If I had to pinpoint the place in camp that shaped my life the most, it is Gund Hall after the meals were served and before everyone was dismissed to the day's activities. Filled with as many camp songs as possible, my child brain soaked them all in. Not just sang them, but absorbed them. To this day, I know in my bones that 'Aardvarks are my Friends,' 'The Princess Pat Lives in a Tree,' and that one day I will 'Build my Castle on the Nile.' I loved when Spazz sang 'Banana Slug' (only once a week—a special occasion) and when, finally, as a CIT, I could stand on the benches and lead them, finally part of the inner circle." The above image is from around 1969, and the below photograph was taken in 1987. (Above, courtesy of Girl Scouts of North East Ohio; below, courtesy of Debbie Kramer.)

In the later 1960s, protest songs such as "Where have all the Flowers Gone?" and "Blowin' in the Wind" came into the song repertoire from counselors who learned them on college campuses. Camp alumna Randy Petkovsek Wooldridge remembers several units camped along the edge of the gas cut "belting out Girl Scout songs in a friendly competition and camaraderie. The songs would echo throughout the valley." (Courtesy of Christine Stark.)

The CIT group set up camp on the western shore of Lake Linnea in 1990 by lashing sticks to trees to create their own camp "furniture." A triumphant high five between Canary (left) and Spif (right) was in order when their kitchen shelf was tested and held up to pressure. (Courtesy of Debbie Kramer.)

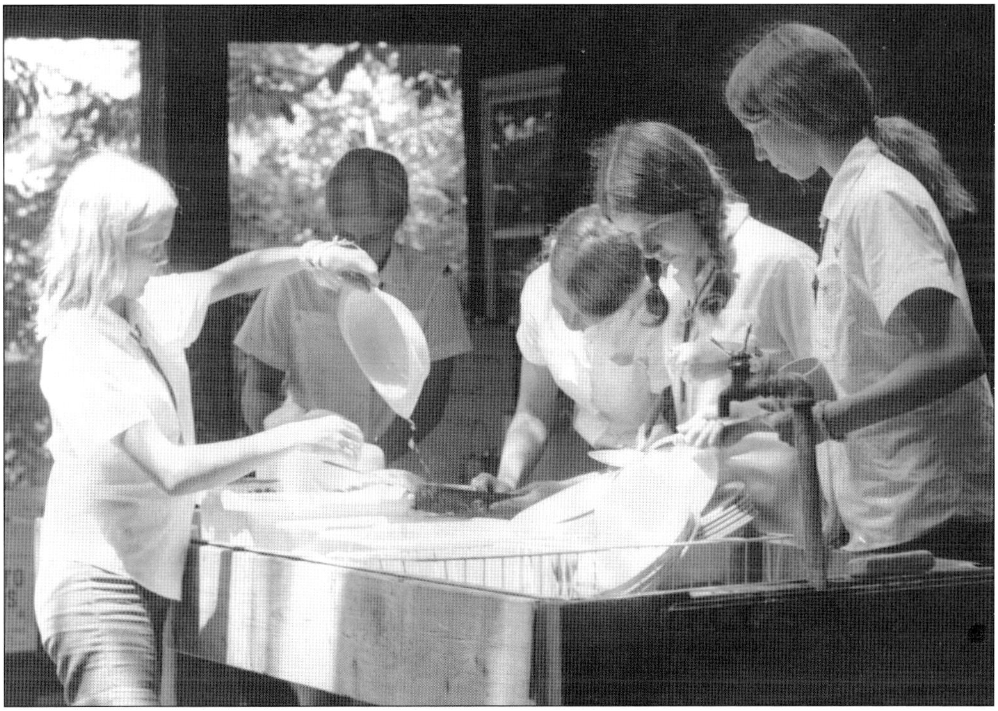

Seely Cabin had a sink on its back porch for cleaning fish or for the usual washing up chores when the girls decided to stay "home" and cook instead of going up to the dining hall. Note the spigot with "rabbit ear" handles. (Courtesy of Girl Scouts of North East Ohio.)

Counselors Tropicana (left) and Cricket (right) light the torches for the final campfire. All the girls gathered at the edge of the lake with "wishboats" to float across the water: a fleet of tiny flames. The songs were solemn with the sadness of impending departure: "On my Honor," "Green Trees/Taps," "Make new friends, but keep the old. One is silver and the other gold." (Courtesy of Dawn Woodward.)

Girl Scout troop camping was all about the planning. Although Kirby House features a beautiful, built-in sideboard in the dining room, it was the set of "Kaper Charts," which were key to weekends like this one in 1999. At troop meetings prior to the campout, patrols planned their menus, divided responsibilities, and made their charts, which were posted in the campsite. (Author's collection.)

The Kirby House dining room is seen here as viewed from the interior balcony. During resident camp, the campers stayed in tents, and Kirby House was reserved for administration and infirmary. But the rest of the year, it was available for troops to rent on weekends. (Author's collection.)

Most cabins had a supply of thin mattresses that were spread out in designated sleeping areas in lieu of beds. (The exceptions were Hilltop House with Murphy beds and Coach House with bunk beds.) Playing on stacks of mattresses was forbidden but often irresistible. Staircase surfing on mattresses was also discouraged. (Courtesy of Debbie Kramer.)

The phone booth in the forest was located just outside of Coach House. It was for authorized emergency use only, although unofficial calls are said to have occurred. It appears jarringly incongruous in this age of cell phones. But at the time, it was a much-appreciated lifeline. (Courtesy of Girl Scouts of North East Ohio.)

Camporees (by various names) were weekend events organized by a service unit (typically all the troops within a defined set of neighborhoods in the city or a school district in the suburbs). Experienced leaders served as role models and mentors for newer leaders. At this camporee in 1998, girls were able to try lemmi sticks on the North House porch under the supervision of trainer Ele Richardson. (Courtesy of Rob Richardson.)

Barb Whitfield (left) teaches outdoor cooking at the fire circle behind Coach House at a 1998 camporee. Core camp was a weekend program started in the 1980s where council staff would be available to provide programming for troops. (Courtesy of Rob Richardson.)

Canadian Girl Guides and American Girl Scouts hold a joint flag ceremony outside Gund Hall at the 1977 international event Catch Today. The council encouraged visits from Girl Scouts and Girl Guides around the world. (Courtesy of Debbie Kramer.)

A costumed folksinger is pictured on the road near Amity House at Kaleidoscope in 1978. Special events could be sponsored by the council or initiated and organized by volunteers. Other special events at Crowell Hilaka include Senior Snowball in 1972, "Doodle-le-doo" Wider Op in 1976, Jazzy Junior Jamboree in 1994, Blue Jeans Benefits in the 1990s, Cadette Roundups, the Cadette/Senior Summit 2003 and 2004, and R.A.I.N.B.O.W.S day camp in 2010. (Courtesy of Girl Scouts of North East Ohio.)

"The Finest Outhouse in All the Land" was established behind the Chagrin Valley Cabin on July 29, 2004, by Girl Scout Troop 1076, led by Donna Kowicki. Ironically, as the girls were working on this construction project, many troop leaders were becoming less willing to accept "primitive" accommodations—without the benefit of indoor plumbing. Camp supporters said that the ability to accept some inconvenience is part of learning to adapt. (Courtesy of Rob Richardson.)

This 1996 sketch map was considered by many to be the definitive map of Crowell Hilaka. It includes the Country Counter (later the Giant Eagle grocery store). Its convenient location right outside the camp gates was not a coincidence but a direct tie to the history of the camp. (Map by Mary Hoyes for Girl Scouts of Lake Erie Council; author's collection.)

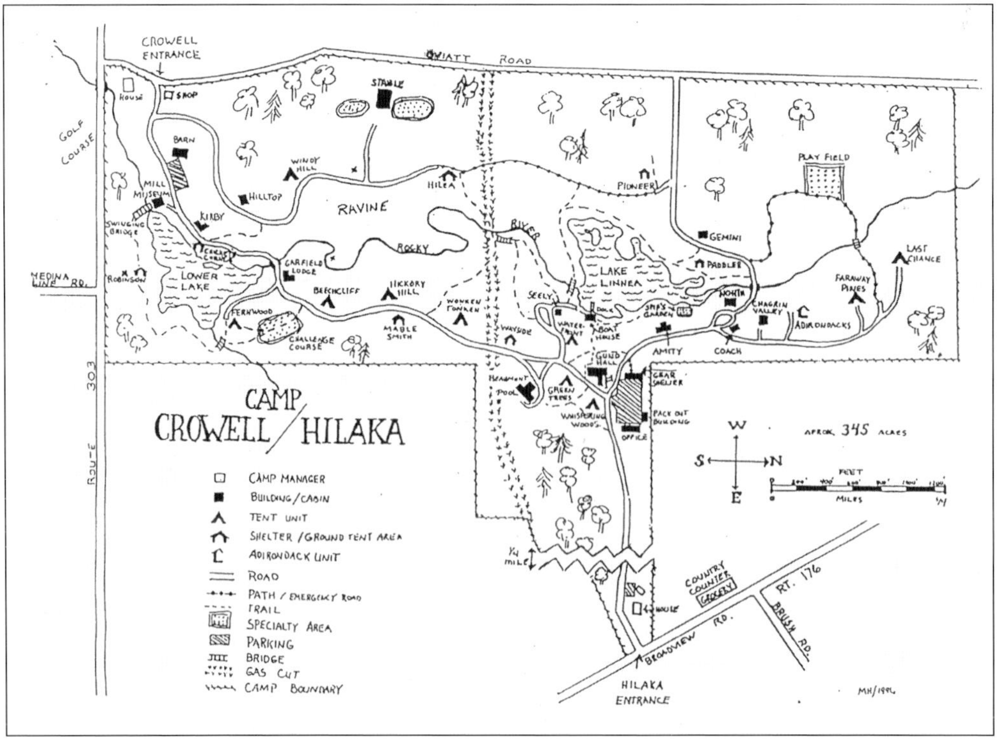

Eight

Ohio's Hidden Treasure, Richfield Heritage Preserve

The national restructuring of Girl Scouting in the early 21st century led to the closure of many camps nationwide, including Crowell Hilaka and three other local camps in 2012. An intricate but fragile chain of events over the next two years led to the preservation of the property by the voters of Richfield. The camp was like a ball volleyed among multiple players and kept aloft in spite of failed attempts and near misses with assists, collaborations, and perseverance. The play started with Girl Scouts of North East Ohio (GSNEO), went to the Western Reserve Land Conservancy (WRLC), then to Friends of Crowell Hilaka (FoCH), to the historical society, to Village Council, back to GSNEO, rebounded to WRLC, back to FoCH, then the Working Group, Village Council, township trustees, Richfield Joint Recreation District, the Richfield Together Campaign, and finally came to rest when the voters said "yes."

When Crowell Hilaka was placed on the market, the highest bid came from the WRLC. Its bid was actually an option, not an outright purchase. Its aim was to hold it temporarily, place a conservation easement on it, and then find another purchaser—an "end user." WRLC searched for a little over a year with no luck. When the clock was running out on the option and with no other end-users in sight, FoCH offered to hold a pledge campaign to raise the $4 million needed to buy the property. Because the camp had been part of the Cleveland Girl Scout Council and Richfield was part of the Akron council's jurisdiction, few people in the neighborhood had ever set foot there. FoCH started its campaign by soliciting endorsements from Richfield Village and Richfield Township. The government officials asked to see the property, and momentum grew from there.

Joe Leslie, WRLC's director of acquisitions in 2013, arranged for FoCH to give tours of the camp to various officials. Meanwhile, FoCH president Corey Ringle gave a tour to representatives from the Buckeye Trail Association (BTA). When BTA saw the property, they pledged $100 an acre to help save it. This pledge, amounting to $36,000, got people's attention and encouraged more pledges. WRLC and FoCH organized a public open house on October 20, 2013. (Courtesy of Joe Leslie.)

By the end of 2013, FoCH was not able to raise the $4 million needed. But working with WRLC and BTA, the organization had shown the property to the people of Richfield, and many had fallen in love with the place. From left to right, Jenny Austin, Lynn Richardson, Corey Ringle, and Lucy Hanigosky from Friends of Crowell Hilaka, with Bob Pond of the Buckeye Trail Association (center), pose near their booth at Richfield's Food Truck Rodeo in 2014. (Author's collection.)

The Richfield Historical Society endorsed FoCH's campaign to save the property. FoCH held a meeting in the Historical Society Museum (pictured here) in November 2013 to plan a strategy. Options were few, but several Richfield citizens who had been to the open house came and expressed their appreciation for the rich history of the property. (Courtesy of Richfield Historical Society.)

Richfield Village councilman Mike Wheeler (left) encouraged WRLC to stay with the effort. Rick Hudak (right), president of the Village Council, encouraged the council to explore options. The Village Council asked WRLC to request an extension on its purchase option. WRLC went ahead and asked GSNEO for more time. (Left, courtesy of Mike Wheeler; right, courtesy of Rick Hudak.)

The GSNEO board was initially reluctant to grant the extension because they hoped to have the property issues settled, and developers who had entered bids in the first round were still interested. Jane Christyson, who was still new as the GSNEO chief executive officer, told the board, "I need you to give those women the time they need to save that camp." With Christyson's encouragement, the board granted the extension. (Courtesy of Jane Christyson.)

FoCH described the camp as a "hidden treasure" to pique curiosity and emphasize its value. At one momentous meeting with WRLC at its Moreland Hills office, Joe Leslie told Corey Ringle, "You need to bring in the village and township officials, or nothing will happen." Ringle had actually brought those very officials to that meeting, at which point she introduced Mike Lyons, Richfield Village Council member, and Lori Pinney, Richfield Township zoning officer. (Courtesy of Friends of Crowell Hilaka.)

Ohio law allowed for a "joint recreation district" to ask voters to approve the purchase of the camp if both township and village governments agreed. Richfield citizen Ralph McNerney sponsored a postcard mailing to Richfield families urging them to contact their government and support the formation of the district. With encouragement from a large number of citizens, the village and township agreed. The Richfield Joint Recreation District (RJRD) was formed in June 2014 to place the issue on the ballot that November. It consisted of, from left to right, Ralph McNerney, Bob Lucas, Floyd Ostrowski, Donna Skoda, Pat Norris, Kelly Clark, and Bill Taylor. They only had one chance to pass a bond issue and operating levy before WRLC's extension expired. They settled on a bond amount of $7.1 million, which would pay for the land and immediate repairs. FoCH pledged to raise additional funds for building restorations. The village provided a meeting space and lent start-up funds. Sandy Apidone and Bobbie Beshara served as cochairs of the political campaign. Karen Smik was the treasurer (P. Wilson, courtesy of *Richfield Times*.)

Terri and Denny Flanagan lent their barn to FoCH for a fundraiser, Music for the Millwheel, which drew local attention to the park. (Courtesy of Rob Richardson.)

Kendrick Chittock was WRLC's project manager for the preservation of Crowell Hilaka. Looking back years later, he reflected on the unique circumstances the campaign presented: "Our greatest weakness was our greatest strength: the fact that so many groups were working together to save the place. So many people had a relationship with this land. One person came in from Florida when we held the open houses. It was incredible." (Courtesy of Kendrick Chittock.)

This postcard was one of four different fliers the campaign mailed out to every household in Richfield. The campaign was intense in part because there had been no real lead time. Major funding for the campaign was contributed by Missy Haslinger. (Author's collection.)

Richfield citizens such as Pat and Sandy Norris (pictured) enthusiastically signed up to help on clean-up day. The camp had been closed for two years, and there was only enough time to do the most rudimentary cosmetic work before the open houses—mowing lawns, raking trails, and sweeping porches. (Author's collection.)

FoCH provided this 22-page guide book to all open house visitors. There were four open houses, and for each, docents were stationed at key points. WRLC and members of the Richfield Together Committee were stationed at Gund Hall to answer voter questions. (Author's collection.)

Campaign workers waited anxiously in the Tavern of Richfield Underground until victory was announced. This grouping included, from left to right, Kelly Clark (peeking around the post), Donna Spiegler, Beth Sanderson, Jenny Austin, Corey Ringle, Lynn Richardson, and campaign cochair Sandy Apidone. Campaign chair Bobbie Beshara and Chris Naizer kneel in front. Richfield voted to buy the property. (Author's collection.)

About the Friends of Crowell Hilaka

Friends of Crowell Hilaka partner with the Richfield Joint Recreation District to preserve, protect, enhance and promote Richfield Heritage Preserve, formerly Camp Crowell Hilaka.

—FoCH mission statement

The Richfield Joint Recreation District (RJRD) is the governing board of Richfield Heritage Preserve (also known as RHP, or simply "the park," or in the National Register of Historic Places as the Camp Crowell Hilaka Historic District), overseeing it for the people of Richfield who bought it in 2015.

Typical of other 501c3 friends' groups, Friends of Crowell Hilaka (FoCH) raises funds for the park to cover what local taxes do not. FoCH is working to stabilize and then restore the major historical structures of RHP. At the time of this writing, our priority is to restore Kirby's Mill. Once the water wheel is turning and new mechanisms for demonstrating hydroelectric power generation are in place, the mill will inspire both appreciation for the past and interest in the science of energy production for the future.

We know there are many more stories of the camp and park than were recorded in this book, and we would love to hear them! If you are interested in contributing your memories of this place, or making a donation to support our mission, you may contact FoCH at friendsofcrowellhilaka.org or FoCH, 100 Wandle Avenue, Bedford, OH 44146.

FoCH is moving toward using the name Friends of Richfield Heritage Preserve. We will also maintain the name Friends of Crowell Hilaka, so our friends can always find us. For the most up to date information, please visit friendsofcrowellhilaka.org.